LEADING WITH SENSE

LEADING
WITH SENSE

The Intuitive Power of
Savoir-Relier

Valérie Gauthier
Foreword by Warren Bennis

STANFORD BUSINESS BOOKS
An Imprint of Stanford University Press
Stanford, California

Stanford University Press
Stanford, California

Special discounts for bulk quantities of Stanford Business Books
are available to corporations, professional associations, and other
organizations. For details and discount information, contact the special
sales department of Stanford University Press. Tel: (650) 736-1782, Fax:
(650) 736-1784

Printed in the United States of America on acid-free, archival-quality paper

Library of Congress Cataloging-in-Publication Data

Gauthier, Valérie, author.
   Leading with sense : the intuitive power of savoir-relier / Valérie
Gauthier; foreword by Warren Bennis.
      pages cm
   Includes bibliographical references and index.
   ISBN 978-0-8047-8625-6 (cloth : alk. paper)
   1. Leadership.   2. Interpersonal relations.   3. Social intelligence.
4. Management.   I. Title.
   HD57.7.G38 2014
   658.4'092—dc23

                                                        2014014042

ISBN 978-0-8047-9272-1 (electronic)

Typeset by Newgen in 10/15 Sabon

CONTENTS

ACKNOWLEDGMENTS

Arriving at this point in writing a book means you are close to closing. But for me there can be no end because this book is a journey where many have been and will be crossing paths in the ongoing quest for understanding and sharing. On these paths I have found unique beings whose support and presence have made this journey a true learning expedition. I wish to thank those people here whether they are flesh and blood or mind and spirit, even though I cannot name all of them.

The book would not exist without Jody Hoffer Gittell, who introduced me to Margo Beth Fleming, whose professional advice, timely encouragements, and acute revisions sharpened every chapter considerably. The bright inputs and insights from Laura McDiarmid helped me complete the work and meet the challenges set by the anonymous reviewers of the manuscript.

My debt also goes to the most inspirational encounters I made over the past decade: Warren Bennis, who as a dear friend kindly agreed to write the book's foreword, and Theodore Zeldin, with whom I have been fortunate to work on and experience shared ideas. Inspiration also came with Edgar Morin, René Girard, and Yves Bonnefoy, who have driven my thoughts all the way, and the poets Mallarmé, Baudelaire, Bishop, Frost, and Whitman, who are the essence of savoir-relier. I also want to thank those who have nourished and illustrated my ideas just by being who they are: Pascal Cagni, Clara Gaymard, and Apollonia Poilâne.

My friend Philippe Gaud has been the attentive ear and presence, always ready to challenge my ideas and open new discussions. My students at HEC Paris, MIT Sloan, and NYU Stern have helped me take a step back from the book while experiencing savoir-relier and putting their own words on the experience. My husband, Danny, has helped rationalize some of that experience.

Finally, the genuine, generous, and generative support of my dear children, Julie and Geoffroy, made this endeavor worth the time and energy. They are the ultimate sense for me, and I dedicate this book to them.

Valérie Gauthier
December 2013

We hear it all the time: the world is moving at a fast pace, shattering our points of reference and our landmarks in time and space. The speed at which complexity is accelerating leaves little room for thinking for ourselves. Dealing with this complexity has become THE challenge. Organizations must embrace globalization to survive; families must compose, decompose, and recompose themselves; individuals must appreciate diverging viewpoints and value diversity. To do so they require a twenty-first-century approach and a new kind of leader, one who can reconcile sense of purpose with business.

Leading with Sense helps us do that. It's a fresh, new, and challenging look at business practices and leadership studies, both individual and organizational, that addresses sense of purpose and relationships with wit and candor. It reconciles effectiveness with integrity, hard work with well-being, people's differences with positive interaction. It brings a sense of respect and understanding for others, including those strongly opposed to others' views.

With a distinct French voice and a twist of American culture, Valérie Gauthier connects views and experiences across the European and North American continents while making global diversity a core component of her approach. Wherever you come from, she opens your mind so that you can find your own path and feel confident about acting on your ideas to create a better future for the world.

The book draws management inspiration from an unlikely source: poets. Poetry carries a universalism that opens the door to every single culture with respect for its uniqueness under the principle of rich and complex language. Poetry is all about delivering a message that provokes emotions, that inspires images and influences ideas, the same way that effective leaders must. I've never seen someone find inspiration for pioneering business practices in poetry, but Valérie makes it seem obvious. Poets interpret symbols for the same purpose as business leaders: to create a sense of belonging and to forge an identity.

This book does the same. It creates links between people's differences and explains why today's world needs light and meaning, intelligence and sensitivity. Leaders must be able to inspire confidence in others. Like poets, they must create a sense of purpose and embody the vision to help those around them build their own paths in the same way.

Today's businesses are looking for executives capable of managing complex situations, fitting into multidisciplinary departments, and steering multicultural teams. In this climate of high demand and higher expectations, mere technical ability is not enough. The ability to understand and collaborate with others, once considered a plus, has become an indispensable qualification. Valérie calls this quality "savoir-relier," or relational know-how. This skill facilitates the development of relationships between individuals, cultures, and ideas. It is a defining characteristic of successful managers.

Further studies, such as the one conducted by Booz Allen Hamilton on recruiters' expectations, confirm the importance of relational intelligence. Companies complain that although many candidates possess sound technical backgrounds and skills, they have difficulty fitting into organizations.

Today, relational intelligence is at the center of a number of theories concerning management and leadership training, including Koestenbaum's Leadership Diamond, MacGregor Burns's model of transactional and transformational leadership, and LMX, or Vertical Dyad Linkage Theory. Concerns over human relations, team building, management, and corporate leadership have all been linked to the notion of relational intelligence.

Born of a reflection on poetry, and the strength of poetic language, the concept of savoir-relier has become the source of a wider reflection on the relationship between people to the world, and especially people to each other. Following the principles developed by British historian and philosopher Theodore Zeldin in his *Intimate History of Humanity*, *Leading with Sense* has chosen to adopt a humanist approach to enable people to develop an understanding of the interpersonal dynamics that shape today's organizations. Applying the principle of savoir-relier requires going beyond the traditional view of a transmission of theories and techniques. While technical and theoretical mastery are essential to the development of a successful manager, viewing real-life management situations through these alone may distort reality and prevent managers from fully addressing problems at hand.

Leadership must be built step by step, through gestures and conversations. Everyone has potential, tolerance, and an ability to listen and understand, but these differ from person to person. It is in this gap that individuals can learn from each other. The greater the difference between that person and yourself, the greater the effort required to understand each other. Growing that understanding builds the trust that will create confident and influential leadership over time. We are seeing the emergence of a new philosophy of management.

This understanding of savoir-relier will lead to a more responsible, intuitive, and human approach to business, which will result in increased balance and productivity. An increasing number of companies are advocating this type of management, which fosters the open exchange of knowledge and experience among co-workers and leads to increased profits. Even more members of Gen Y are looking for meaning in their jobs and in the companies they will join. Thanks to this novel approach, the savoir-relier mind-set with its genuine, generous, and generative characteristics will certainly open avenues for new and enriched business practices.

I   SAVOIR-RELIER

A Sustainable, Sense-Based Approach to Leadership

My first official leadership experience in a business setting began the day that I was elected to become associate dean of the MBA Program at HEC Paris, the leading business school in France. I had spent the previous ten years as a professor of English and communication there, developing partnerships with U.S. schools to help HEC become an international player and recruiting professors and assistants, but I had never really led or managed a program or a team. My new position placed me at the head of a dramatically failing program with angry students, demoralized staff, and a drop in international rankings. From that starting point, I had to turn this MBA into a program that would be respected worldwide.

My plan was to recruit internationally, redesign the curriculum, and reach out to the companies that would recruit our graduates. My success would be judged on progress in these areas, but the real challenge lay elsewhere: I could not achieve any of these objectives alone. I was going to lead a team, a demoralized team. And I had no leadership or management training, just a sense of mission, and a drive to improve the lives of the students who would be recruited to and graduate from our program.

My first instinct was to listen and observe. I met with each member of the staff, empathizing with the stories and feelings that they were willing to share. As I learned the history of the program and heard about the tensions that had driven it to its current, difficult position, I began to comprehend the magnitude of the challenge I was facing. The only solution was to fight with courage and patience and, step by step, to rebuild the morale of the people involved by introducing a sense of purpose, a direction, a rationale, and a lot of common sense into our day-to-day activities. Taking account of the students' concerns and the staff's perceptions of the situation, I was going to build sense and re-create positive relationships. I was going to use savoir-relier.

SAVOIR-RELIER: AN ACT, A CAPACITY, A MIND-SET, AND A PROCESS

I believe that leadership is not a technique: it is a state of being that translates into acts. It is in his or her acts of leadership that the leader exists.

Savoir-relier—pronounced savwaʀ ʀəlje—is an expression that I came up with in 1994 as part of a project to define new paradigms for the education of twenty-first-century leaders and managers. *Savoir* means "to know" and "knowledge"; by extension, it means know-how, to know how to be. *Relier* means the capacity to connect, relate, link, and, by extension, rely on other people and on oneself. The expression can be roughly translated as "relational intelligence," although the original French also captures notions of knowledge and capacity.

Savoir-relier is a way to work from tensions by taking critical dimensions of leadership such as trust, resilience, agility, intuition, courage, and complexity and leveraging them to enhance our capacity to navigate the increasingly complex and highly relational world we live in. It is a type of leadership that is marked by humility and intuition,[1] recognizing the importance of human relationships and the value of diversity as a means to drive innovation and performance. It is a tool for approaching and managing complex problems at individual, interpersonal, organizational, and institutional levels.

Savoir-relier is an act: the act of generating sensible and sustainable relations between different or divergent entities to build sense for individuals and organizations alike. When developed at the individual level, savoir-relier is a capacity. Savoir-relier leaders use their analytical and emotional capacities to build stronger, better connections among members of an organization. They build sense from existing patterns by creating new ones and encouraging initiative and autonomy. When it is adopted across an organization, savoir-relier becomes a mind-set, which generates a collective identity.

Applied to problem-solving or decision-making issues, savoir-relier underscores a process called the *relational circuit*, which can be used to generate and regenerate the vision, sense, and energy required to keep pace with today's challenges. The relational circuit serves as a guiding tool. It helps leaders reorganize the relationships between different elements in a system in order to uncover innovative solutions to problems. It takes the pieces of a jigsaw puzzle and rearranges them, even adds some new pieces, to create a coherent and consistent—and renewed—whole.

Managing the Challenge of Change

Savoir-relier in all its incarnations can empower leaders to rise and face challenges, which so often come as calls for change. The disastrous state of the HEC MBA meant change was a necessity. I was ready for it and thought I could take everyone with me to meet the challenge.

This was my first mistake. Some people would not—or could not—embrace the adaptation, stress, uncertainty, and new horizons before us. I had to make difficult decisions and help members of the team who preferred safety and stability to move into departments that weren't making an active and urgent shift to an international way of thinking, working, and behaving: language, technology, and diversity were our main drivers for change. Students were arriving from all over the world. Competition from other programs was becoming tougher. We were working in an environment of raised expectations and increased professionalism while also struggling to become more international.

My second set of mistakes came along as I recruited new people to the team. Sometimes I rushed and simply recruited staff with the wrong profiles because of the pressure to improve services as quickly as possible. Sometimes the integration phase for a new person on the team worked so well that I completely let go and lost contact and control. During my eight years in charge of the program, I came to realize that for the team to work well, every person on it needed attention and care. I understood that success was not just about the results but also how each individual member of the team took part in the process and *felt* about that success. Success was about how people engaged in the process of change. In this second lesson, I found another use for savoir-relier: it served as a lens I could use to understand the dynamics of my team.

The more we move toward a service society, the more human capital becomes the source of corporate success. Savoir-relier focuses on human relationships and human diversity as a means to drive innovation and collective performance. It helps managers use their innate senses to make connections and find common ground between all sorts of things: employees of different races and ages, workers in different functional units, teams in different regions. It nurtures relationships between people, ideas, cultures, and generations.

Building sensible, positive, trustworthy relationships between entities that are inherently different, opposite, or antagonistic requires skill, determination, and dedication; fostering attitudes that value difference and generate mindful innovations within complex dynamic systems is not a straightforward task. But the returns—whether they are counted in terms of profits, patents, or the quality of the working environment—make it worthwhile.

Building for the Long Term
The turnaround in the fortunes of the HEC MBA was considerable and sustainable: the program moved from sixty-seventh to a stable eighteenth position in the *Financial Times* ranking in just five years; class sizes increased from 120 students per class to 230 students per class in seven years; the quality and diversity of the students improved in incredible ways.

Some people were left on the side of the road or simply left the team because they could not or did not want to be a part of that change. The toughest part of my leadership was to fire and recruit. The greatest reward was to see staff and students feel proud to be part of the program, which had become part of their identity, of their sense of purpose.

When I was able to connect effectively with the majority of my team, all was well. The ties that bound us were the sense of purpose I was able to demonstrate, the energy I was able to instill, the direction I was able to show, the example I was able to set. The inherent motivations for people to engage and commit to their job were simple things like "my colleagues' smiles when I go to work in the morning," and "nice people and a nice place to be," apparently mundane ideas but indicators of a harmonious workplace where tensions were managed and positive feelings came to the fore. Through savoir-relier, I had created an environment where people could feel happy in their work, focus on results, and confidently suggest and implement improvements.

I learned along the way that I could not please everybody and that there would always be someone, somewhere, to oppose or dislike every decision and every idea. It was important and good to accept those divergent views and include them in my plans because, to connect, I had to learn what was disconnected. To build and create something new, one begins with dissociated or misaligned components. Savoir-relier led me and can lead you to build something new that will generate value and sense for the long term.

LEVERAGING SIMPLICITY TO MANAGE COMPLEXITY

The demands and challenges of the twenty-first century and beyond are neither static nor linear. Globalism and the speed at which information is exchanged, both of which give rise to complexity, are central to these challenges. We also face more elemental challenges. After the shock of Hurricanes Katrina and Irene, for example, Hurricane Sandy hit the United States on October 29, 2012, shutting down Wall Street for two consecutive days and killing at least ninety people in the United States alone. It caused damage estimated at $50 billion and left more than eight million homes without power, some of which remained cut off for weeks. For the most powerful economy in the world to suffer, in 2012, such catastrophic domino effects from a natural disaster illustrates the need for leadership strategies to incorporate mechanisms that take account of complexity. When dealing with theoretical chaos or the reality of a world that can be uncertain, unpredictable, scary, and volatile, we need a new paradigm for leadership. We need to find ways to leverage simplicity to manage increasingly complex and unpredictable situations. We need to develop an approach that uses sense to underpin sustainable success. Let's start by understanding how our thinking about complexity in organizations has evolved.

The Evolution of Organizational Complexity

When Raymond E. Miles and his colleagues explored economic and organizational evolution from the late 1800s onward, they identified three
eras: Standardization, Customization, and Innovation.[2] Each era had a
corresponding organizational model and core capabilities. Standardization, which reigned until the 1920s, had the U-form, a "unitary" centralized approach with vertically integrated functional structures that relied
on planning and control. Customization, prevalent from the 1920s to the
1980s, was based on the M-form: multidivisional, with matrix structures,
and relying on delegation. The I-form, which emerged in the 1980s, uses
multifirm networks and community-based structures, relies on collaboration, and is named in honor of innovation.

Once General Motors had pioneered the matrix organization, almost
every large U.S. firm started using the M-form to structure their business
operations. The I-form evolved when those firms started to experiment
with variations on M-form organizational designs and share this knowledge spontaneously. The I-form itself is now evolving as companies experiment with new designs of collaborative networks and communities, driven
by entrepreneurial R&D and, of course, the Internet, which has made it
possible to collaborate beyond the limitations of geographical proximity.

The I-form provides organizational structures that respond to the challenges of an increasingly complex world. In this complex, fast-moving,
hyperconnected world, the role of leaders appears more limited than in
more traditional U-form and M-form models: leaders do not control the
emergent processes. Instead, as patterns emerge, individuals must make
sense of their complex, dynamic environments. They must facilitate social
interactions and foster interpersonal structures that, in turn, generate new
structures and further transform the organization.

The Changing Context of Leadership

Savoir-relier prepares leaders for this evolving I-form world, enabling them
to embrace that which is unfamiliar, distant, original, and new—to engage
uncertainty and open up a wide spectrum of otherwise hidden knowledge.
By addressing leadership from a relational perspective and tying it to sense,
savoir-relier can help managers to thrive in ever more complex environ-

ments and problems. Tensions and paradoxes can be leveraged to generate sustainable and trustworthy relationships at work; autonomy and freedom, coupled with frameworks and structures, can lead to mindful innovation.

The research undertaken by Miles and his colleagues suggests that historically, we have considered leadership as a linear leader-follower process, centered in personalities and relying on authority. However, when it comes to complexity, we need a different line of thought, one where the top-down models of leadership are challenged by the tensions between internal, self-generative influence and external forces. Although many business books use models and praise the excellence of companies on the grounds of self-defined performance criteria, what we need to succeed in a complex world cannot be packaged as a straightforward roadmap.

Let's consider three business books from the last three decades that tried to identify the factors that underpinned the success of high-performing companies and, importantly, quantify those factors in such a way that other companies, other leaders, could apply them and achieve similar results. As we will see, they fell short because their "one size fits all" approach failed to account for a mix of complexity and human relationships.

In Search of Excellence, by Tom Peters and Robert Waterman, was published in 1982. The authors analyzed forty-three companies, all of which were Fortune 500 companies and among the consulting firm McKinsey's best-performing clients. They identified eight common themes in the companies' approach to business: a bias for action; proximity to the customer; autonomy and entrepreneurship; productivity through people; a hands-on, value-driven management philosophy that guides everyday practice; a focus on established areas of business; a simple form and lean staff; and simultaneous autonomy on the shop floor but in a context of shared core values). These themes have become lessons for managers and leaders who thrive for excellence in their business. But on what grounds?

Peters's personal driver was to prove how crucial people are to business success. He advocated instinct and gut feeling to run businesses, which was a major shift in analyzing business success at the time and partly accounts for the lasting success of the book. However, despite his success in railing against the "hard factors" and his arguments in favor of human relationships and simplicity, his attempts to tie those factors down into a replicable, cookie-cutter formula for success meant he ended up replacing the old metrics with a different, but similarly rigid, approach. The book's short list of forty-three large successful American organizations such as Walt Disney Company, 3M, and IBM yet excluded some—General Electric, for instance—on the basis of quantitative measures used for the selection. Agreeably, the eight lessons remain a good reference for doing business today. They advocate values and actions that apply to effective business. However, they do not address the issues of geopolitics, diversity, or cross-continent mergers and acquisitions that make global, large, and small companies shiver and fall nowadays. General Electric, for instance, has grown its business with success outside the eight lessons drawn from *In Search of Excellence*.

In 1994, *Built to Last* made its way onto the best-seller lists. Based on historical research and survey responses from CEOs, Jim Collins and Jerry Porras selected eighteen companies that had outperformed the general market for decades and that they considered "visionary." Their definition of "visionary" was rather encompassing, as Jennifer Reingold and Ryan Underwood contend in their article for *Fast Company*: "A visionary company doesn't simply balance between preserving a tightly held core ideology and stimulating vigorous change and movement; it does both to the extreme."[3] Again, the authors tried to distill the essential principles that made those companies "visionary" and to identify what set them apart from their less successful peers.

Ten years later, almost half of the visionary companies on the list had dropped dramatically in performance and reputation. The problem was that Collins and Porras had tried to scientifically measure qualities that don't lend themselves to quantification. How do you measure vision? Can you equate success with shareholder return? Although these reservations were raised publicly, the book was a huge success. Once again, the measures, the numbers, and the recipes all reassured anxious leaders and managers that their problems could be solved if they just found the right system.

Good to Great, published in 2001, was yet another attempt to identify the factors that allow some companies to outperform their market and their industry. Jim Collins ranked 1,435 companies as "good" based on their performance over the previous forty years; of these, 11 were classed as "great." Collins identified seven factors that other companies wishing to embark on the road to "greatness" could apply to their own operations.

Twelve years later, when the same performance criteria were applied to the same companies, only one of the original eleven "great" companies was still outperforming the market. The others had disappeared, been bought, or seen their stocks fall or stagnate. Once again, history had shown that solutions that work at one time don't work forever and that best practices are not static. The challenges of doing business today are more than a match for prescriptive methodologies and metrics.

Although these books met with great success and advanced the debate on corporate management and leadership, they ultimately failed to pinpoint what makes companies thrive over time with respect to individual and collective well-being and sense of purpose. As we will see later, the authors were sense-makers rather than sense-builders, exploring the reality of past or present situations rather than drawing out ideas that could be projected into future situations. They sought to identify a domino effect, to establish linear relationships that would enable leaders to reproduce the same sequences with the same results over and over again. In doing so, they failed to take account of the complexity that is inherent to everyday life and to business.

If theories built around linear relationships are too simplistic to make sense of the real world, how well do theories built around nonlinearity cope? The butterfly effect, black swan theory, feedback loops, and the irrationality of desire provide interesting insights for leaders seeking to achieve complex goals in unpredictable environments.

The Butterfly Effect. "The butterfly effect" is the familiar expression used to describe the disproportionate impact that a minor change at one point in a deterministic nonlinear system can have on a later state. In the classic example, the formation of a hurricane is said to be contingent on whether a butterfly had flapped its wings on another continent several weeks before. In leadership, the butterfly effect can help us understand how human relationships, which may appear minor within the larger context of a company and its systems and processes, can have a significant impact on outcomes. Minor alterations in relationships can take on a viral form that amplify and modify our mind-set and those of people around us. When the original ingredients induce positive feelings and behaviors, the resulting actions improve performance and well-being.

The "butterfly" can be something as simple as a conversation. At one executive seminar on the savoir-relier protocol, for example, I applied simple diversity criteria to pair up participants for an exercise. One pair was composed of two men: one headed the finance business unit in the United States, and the other was head of operations in Germany. The exercise created a strong sense of trust and they discovered that they had undergone similar traumatic experiences in the course of their lives, which had given them a sense of resilience and determination. While discussing broader challenges within their company, one of them proposed that they should work together to launch a joint U.S.-German initiative. A year after the seminar, their idea had been transformed into a ten-year contract for the company that generates $150,000 in annual profit.

Black Swan Theory.   Nassim Nicholas Taleb's acclaimed book, *The Black Swan*,[4] shows the limits of statistics in the face of the unpredictable. Black swan events are identified by three characteristics: they are a surprise, they have a major effect, and they are rationalized by hindsight. If we had captured the right data we could have anticipated and possibly prevented the events. Black swans are particularly interesting because they apply as much to large events, such as September 11 or the Black Monday financial crash of 1987, as to individual and personal events. Taleb notes that black swans are subjective and depend on the observer; what may be a black swan surprise for a turkey is not a black swan surprise to its butcher. Our goal is to avoid being the turkey by identifying areas of vulnerability and taking preventive action in advance of the butcher's arrival.

A savoir-relier mind-set improves our ability to cope with black swans; it develops our ability not only to make sense of current circumstances but also to build sense from those foundations and project that sense into the future. As Taleb explains, "If you want to get an idea of a friend's temperament, ethics, and personal elegance, you need to look at him under the tests of severe circumstances, not under the regular rosy glow of daily life. Can you assess the danger a criminal poses by examining only what he does on an ordinary day? Can we understand health without considering wild diseases and epidemics? Indeed the normal is often irrelevant. Almost everything in social life is produced by rare but consequential shocks and jumps; all the while almost everything studied about social life focuses on the 'normal,' particularly with bell curve methods of inference that tell you close to nothing. Why? Because the bell curve ignores large deviations, cannot handle them, yet makes us confident that we have tamed uncertainty."[5]

Savoir-relier pushes us to be more vigilant and observant, more mindful of our environment and our relationships, more aware of the fact that many events occur outside our models simply because many events are without precedent and most relationships are not linear.

Feedback Loops.   A third interesting concept is that of feedback, particularly feedback loops. Feedback is a process that allows observation and information about an action to influence the same action in the present or future. A feedback loop, then, allows feedback and self-correction to adapt actions according to differences between the actual output and the desired output.

The notion of feedback arises repeatedly in any discussion of savoir-relier as exchange and return make an important contribution to our ability to develop awareness and adapt to our environment. In communication, for example, feedback loops facilitate the appreciation of both positive and critically constructive feedback. Feedback facilitates changes in behavior and introduces systems that enable us to understand, control, and enhance performance on the basis of successes and failures, experiments and actions, both positive and negative. Savoir-relier can induce positive innovation and change by driving feedback through sensing (observing and listening), resilience (learning from failure), and sense making (explaining and adapting).

The Irrationality of Desire.   Applied to human behavior, particularly desire, the concepts of nonlinearity and feedback bring another dimension to our understanding of relationships. René Girard, professor at Stanford University, argues that the subject-object relationship is not linear.[6] Under the guise of this assumption, each person freely directs his or her desire toward an object that possesses an inherent value that explains this desire. For example, my desire for an iPhone might be explained by its technological and social utility and aesthetic design. We assume that our desire for a certain object, whether a person, a house we want to buy, or our next step on the career ladder, is the result of free choice.

This linear vision is clear and simple, but it does not explain more complex features of desire, such as envy or jealousy. In reality, we envy the person who possesses the desired object, while the object itself is only of relative importance. Girard identifies a completely new mechanism of human desire by suggesting the existence of a third element, a mediator of desire, which is "the other." As he puts it, "It is because the person I have taken as a model desires a particular object that I, in turn, desire the object." In other words, the subject's desire for a particular object stems from a relationship or rivalry with the person who possesses it.

Advertising, for example, rarely shows us objects as desirable in themselves but instead showcases attractive people who desire the product or appear to be fulfilled by possessing it. The relationships we develop are nurtured by desire, which is a complex and fundamental motivation for human action. Although it is often described as an emotion, I would argue that desire is a sense and that it has more in common with a bodily function, comparable to the need for food. It is an interesting element to address in understanding relationships and their inherent complexity. With mimetic desire, for instance, we can develop an approach to marketing that deliberately integrates the need that consumers have to mimic others and adapt to profound human needs. Feedback loops inform desire and create complexity, again demonstrating the need for a nonlinear approach to decision making and problem solving.

Understanding How Complexity Keeps Relationships in Motion
While the butterfly effect, black swan theory, feedback loops, and the irrationality of desire help us interpret and better envision complexity, they do not explore our personal experience of complexity. We connect to the world around us through sensations, emotions, and thoughts. These physical, emotional, and intellectual responses to reality have a profound effect on our reactions to reality. In addition to the relationship that we build with the physical world, our life is defined by the relationships we

have with the people around us (parents, siblings, friends, children, peers, and the like), by the events we experience, and by the places where these events and relationships unfold. We need savoir-relier because the world is complex, but we also need it because our lives are relational.

Herein lies the leadership challenge. Leaders are the link between the individual and the organization; a good leader needs to weave together the motivations of one with the needs of the other. This apparently simple line of thought masks, of course, a complex reality: tensions subtend all relationships. Building sense out of those tensions, those relationships, is, therefore, critical to effective leadership. Sense can transform our relationships by helping us understand underlying tensions and harness them in a positive way. This implies a necessary dive into both the individual and the organizational dimensions. A psychological lens helps us focus on the individual or micro aspect of leadership, looking at the roles, personality, and characteristics of the savoir-relier leader. A sociological lens filters the collective and organizational dimensions, producing insights about structure, networks, functions, strategy, and group identity.

Whereas existing theories attempt to find or force linear relationships,[7] even when they acknowledge the need to engage across hierarchies, savoir-relier tackles complexity by valuing the importance of interactions and interconnectedness between antagonistic or paradoxical entities. As Heraclitus put it more than 2,500 years ago, "Unite whole and part, agreement and disagreement, accordant and discordant; from all comes one, and from one all."[8] Pascal echoed him centuries later: "Since everything is . . . dependent and supporting, mediate and immediate, and all is held together by a natural though imperceptible chain, which binds together things most distant and most different, I hold it equally impossible to know the parts without a knowledge of the whole as it is to know the whole without knowing the parts in detail."[9]

In more recent times, Edgar Morin has sought to resolve the challenge of complexity by binding order and disorder through interactions that find common ground between opposites.[10] Morin underpinned his approach with three principles: dialogic, recursive, and holographic.[11] The dialogic principle emphasizes a special kind of link where the elements that are necessary to each other are both complementary and antagonistic.

In business, this principle serves the notion of dialogue that is so crucial to decision making, consensus, teamwork, or any form of interaction between workers, managers, and customers. Morin's recursive principle dictates that when individuals produce society, society in turn produces individuals. In business, the recursive principle can be applied to teamwork and highlights the value of shared responsibility where each individual has an impact on the team's results, which in turn will affect each individual.

Morin's third principle, the holographic principle, surpasses both reductionism and holism by relying on the image of the hologram. Morin uses examples from the biological and sociological worlds to explain: "Each cell of our organism contains the totality of the genetic information of that organism"; seemingly "the sociologist is part of the society of which s/he is not the center, but a part and possessed by all society" and "we human beings know the world through the messages that our senses transmit to our brains. The world is present inside our minds, which are inside the world."[12] This view implies that leadership roles are not the exclusive domain of one individual or position but are present in every individual who has a responsibility toward the collective entity where he or she operates. Everyone is a full member of the company and embodies the corporate values, culture, and identity that make an organization what it is. In this respect, the convergence of individual and collective sense makes the system work.

On the shoulders of these intellectual giants, we can build the three principles to make sense of complex thinking: our knowledge of the parts is enriched by our knowledge of the whole, which in turn draws from knowledge of the parts. The bonds formed in this process are the illustration of the capacity and will to build relationships in a complex circuit (embodied by the notion of savoir-relier). These ties that bind us are the drivers of sense.

Balancing Structure and Freedom
The world needs savoir-relier because problems are not objects. A problem is a pattern, a series of movements, an element in a bigger picture that exists only through its interactions with its environment. Successful lead-

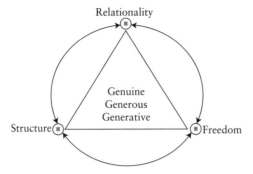

FIGURE I.I   Relationality as a balance between structure and freedom

ers are those who maintain the delicate balance between movement and permanence, between structure and freedom.

Savoir-relier takes the standard oppositional relationship between structure and freedom and transforms it into a strong and functional triangular relationship with the addition of relationality, as shown in Figure 1.1. Relationality is characterized by perception, reliance, resilience, and responsibility.

This triangular framework creates an environment within which leaders and organizations can operate. With this setting established, a leader's focus switches to the qualities and processes that guide behavior and decisions. Savoir-relier promotes behavior that is genuine, generous, and generative because these positive expressions of relationality are possible only when the foundations of perception, reliance, resilience, and responsibility are in place. Perception associated with a genuine mind-set that breeds self-awareness and confidence emphasizes the relationship between you and yourself at the heart of the living ecosystem. Reliance, combined with the collaboration and trust that builds on a generous mind-set, emphasizes the relationships between you and others. Finally, resilience and responsibility, alongside a generative mind-set that breeds innovation and influence, play an effective sense-relational leadership role by emphasizing the relationships between you and your organization as well as with society at large. In later chapters we will explore these qualities and principles, and the relational circuit that drives decision making, from both an individual and an organizational perspective.

Savoir-relier complements and builds on relevant models, such as transformational leadership, situational leadership, and relational coordination. It depends on a cross-disciplinary approach, drawing on poetry, philosophy, sociology, psychology, and linguistics. In the process, it provides us with a meaningful response to a complicated question: How can leadership reinvent itself to meet the demands and challenges of the twenty-first century and beyond?

Acknowledging the Power of Intuition, Experience, and Sensory Perception

In 2001, I went on a ski expedition in the French Alps with Régis, a senior guide who was born and raised in the region and whose father and grandfather were mountain guides. The weather predictions and snow conditions were good, with a solid six feet of snow from previous weeks of snowfall. It was February, at the heart of the ski season. The wind was blowing at forty miles an hour, which is common for the area, and although the temperatures were slightly higher than usual it was nothing significant. As we were making our way up the mountain with our climbing skins attached to our skis, moving slowly across heavy snow, I was thinking ahead to the moment that I would enjoy the downhill, my motivation for this expedition to 9,500 feet. After three hours of climbing, Régis suddenly stopped and urged us to move sideways to a place where rocks had formed a natural shelter. We immediately did as we were told; the order was clear and we trusted our guide's decisions. A few seconds later an avalanche took off way above our position and headed in our direction at incredible speed.

The guide's sensible and subjective experience of the situation saved us. He had heard the growling sound early enough and felt the vibrations under his skis. His body had told him that the avalanche was coming even though nothing in the weather forecast, the snow conditions, or the topology of the area would have enabled him to predict it on a purely rational basis. Just as an animal senses the storm coming and starts shaking way before human ears can hear it, the guide's vigilance and his extensive experience of the mountains, accumulated over many years, was the source of the instant decision to move everyone sideways and away from the avalanche before it even started and in time to save us all. Many have encountered similar moments when a primary sense drives our decisions, both in life and in business.

The primary sense that my guide experienced is often called "intuition"; I believe it is too often cast aside. Why do we fear or discount what our senses tell us when they can save our lives? In part it is because sensibility and sensitivity are somehow confused with sentimentalism, which is used disparagingly to refer to people who are victims of their feelings. When hard facts, data, and rationalization rule in business, no one wants to be perceived as soft or weak or sentimental. Subjectivity is also feared because it is confused with being partial or biased. Being emotional is confused with being emotive. But what if we were to reexamine these assumptions? What if we were to consider sensory input as data?

Our senses are central to our ability to understand the reality of our experience at any given moment. It is important to note not only the distinction between our senses and our emotions, but also the difference between sensibility, namely our ability to perceive sensory data, and sensitivity, which relates to our response or reaction to those stimuli. Sensibility enables us to be receptive and reactive to the signals coming our way, which gives way to sensitivity, which in turn results in perception—that is, the cognitive capacity to understand and decode the world through our senses. This apparently subtle distinction is important because of the learning component inherent in this process. Indeed, sensibility, or mindfulness as Karl Weick calls it,[13] can be enhanced by simple exercises that connect us to reality. Sensibility can also become a state of mind that helps us apprehend complexity. Both sensibility and sensitivity will be discussed in detail in later chapters.

BUILD CONFIDENCE, INSPIRE TRUST
Becoming a Savoir-Relier Leader

Savoir-relier can be developed and grown with practice and determination. By developing savoir-relier, a leader builds the confidence necessary to make sound decisions that are the result of consultations, exchange, and debates. When employed with courage, empathy, humility, and resilience, savoir-relier stimulates creative initiatives and generates sense that drives action and results. Savoir-relier leaders are not just the CEOs or executives; they are everywhere in the organization.

What If Your Company Were Like a Horse?
To me, horsemanship is a good illustration of the need for balance in strong, effective working relationships—balance between structure and freedom, control and autonomy, technical skills and emotional connections. Physically, you are no match for a powerful animal like a horse, but with the right intellectual approach and the right techniques you can find yourself holding the reins and working in harmony with a strong and willing partner.

Take yourself through the steps involved in building such a relationship. It starts with words, with the sound of your voice; then, once the horse is close, it becomes a question of touch and smell. The horse will sense whether you are nervous or confident, happy or irritable, and react accordingly. Subtle, unspoken messages, transmitted through body language, are already influencing the direction the relationship will take.

Once you're in the saddle, the means of control become more obvious—the reins and stirrups are visible symbols—but the mechanisms of control remain subtle: a little finger can decide a turn while a very slight move of the heel and calf can determine speed and direction. If your grip is too strong, the horse will rebel and get tough and tense; too loose a grip will leave the horse uncertain and wild. The aim is for him to be under your control but able to express his power and grace freely. Every move you make will affect that outcome. The balance between control and freedom that you are able to establish will influence the degree to which the partnership is successful or unsuccessful. With hard work, skill, and trust, you will be able to build a relationship that makes it all look easy, in which the energy flows and the onlooker sees only effortless power and grace.

I believe that successful leadership requires a similarly harmonious balance between control and freedom. The effort a savoir-relier leader invests in building relationships, in establishing trust, will be repaid in the form of a successful organization that flows. An old-fashioned, authoritarian leader might be able to achieve equally good or better financial results in the short term, but over the long term, the benefits of building sense and strong relationships will come to the fore. Furthermore, just as there would be no joy in riding a broken-spirited horse that was controlled by force alone, so there is no joy in leading a demotivated or demoralized team.

It is the leader's responsibility to use the right techniques to engage each person in a way that speaks to her, to respect her as an individual, to place trust and confidence in her ability to work effectively with the right guidance. My experience in turning around the HEC MBA program, in reviving its broken spirit, taught me the importance and exhilaration of reaching a healthy gallop. It is my hope that this book will take you on a similar ride.

In the next chapter, we will meet three adept riders—inspirational leaders of a new generation whose genuine, generous, and generative natures have enabled them to achieve great success.

2 THE SAVOIR-RELIER LEADER
A Portrait

Clara Gaymard is president and CEO of General Electric in France and vice president of GE International. She is also the mother of nine children. She believes that "considering yourself as an undivided and genuine whole is a way to start changing your view about your role and to accept the benefit of transferring knowledge and experience from one sphere of life to another."[1]

Many argue that relationships between the professional and personal sides of a leader's life create complications and that they should stay separate. Gaymard believes this is a false argument, an excuse to draw a line between the two and to avoid looking inside yourself: "Your personal life can bring responses to your professional issues just as your professional experience can help your personal life. They nurture one another. I feel much stronger in my leadership role today because I know I can rely on what I learned from my experience raising my kids while pursuing my career."[2] Gaymard's confidence is central to her ability to be a genuine savoir-relier leader. The authenticity and transparency with which she lives her life equips her to navigate her complex environment, both personal and professional, through relationships based on trust, candor, and acceptance. The first milestone of the savoir-relier leader is genuineness, which paves the way to a leadership of sense. Being genuine then combines

with generous and generative behaviors to build strong and positive relationships between people and things. Let's now illustrate each of the 3 Gs
with living examples.

BEING GENUINE: USING HONESTY AND CANDOR TO WORK WITH TENSIONS
Confidence, Autonomy, and Authenticity

Being genuine begins with being true to yourself—not an easy task when,
as a leader, you are asked to take on many roles in different situations with
varied audiences. Being a whole person is the first thing that will help you
shoulder the roles and responsibilities that come with leadership positions.
For some, leadership begins with being the elder in a family, or the captain
of a sports team, or a parent. Indeed, raising children requires many leadership qualities because it is a complex and challenging task where nothing is
ever certain: children grow and change constantly in unpredictable ways.
Parents must anticipate, adapt, listen, observe, lead the way, and give the
best of themselves to nurture and equip their children to live and play a
positive role. Perception, reliance, resilience, and responsibility, our four
relationality principles, certainly apply to parenthood.

Confidence is a fundamental leadership skill that Gaymard developed
as a parent. She believes that being a genuine sense-relational leader means
growing your own self-confidence first and then helping others to grow.
One example she gives is teaching each of her kids how to cross the street
alone to go and buy bread at age five. In this act of education, she was
giving them the key to the autonomy that a large family requires. But she
was also overcoming her fear of letting go by building their confidence.

She explains how this translates to her leadership style: "In the organization, you want to generate shared responsibility, and that comes with
autonomy."[3] Today we know that autonomy can stimulate innovation.
Google has understood this and allows its engineers to work on anything
they want for 20 percent of their time. When you know that about half
of Google's products, such as Gmail, are generated during that time, it is
easy to understand the value of autonomy.

But it takes time for people to feel confident enough to act autono-
mously. "You have to take your child by the hand and cross the street with

him or her many times, explaining how to wait for the light to turn red and watch for the crosswalk signal. I know it is time well invested because it is the best way for your child to build the self-confidence they need to cross the street alone. It also allows you to let go and overcome your own fears. This confidence to let go and allow others do their own thing is the first step toward the sense of responsibility that both parent and child, or boss and employee, require if they are to develop a relationship based on trust. That trust results in an effective delegation of tasks and missions."[4]

Being able to transfer experience from one sphere to the other while remaining your true self is a sign of genuineness. Gaymard's confidence in her lived experiences at home opened her up to this practice in her leadership role at work. Likewise, candor can facilitate a person's ability to take action as a whole person in his or her professional life.

Candor—transparency combined with personal integrity and high ethical standards—has been praised in recent years as a way to improve performance.[5] Transparency, straight talk,[6] and honesty are described as tools to create a "culture of candor" that proves effective in the face of boundless organizations and complex environments. For example, in a NASA experiment described by scholars Warren Bennis and James O'Toole, space shuttle pilots who made the right choices in difficult moments were those who engaged in open, candid exchanges of information with their crews.[7] A "decisive" leadership style, on the other hand, resulted in a crew whose members felt hesitant to intervene and contribute as fully as possible. More than an attitude, candor is a mind-set, a permanent way of interacting with people on a daily basis, as well as the expression of a deliberate desire to share information. Being candid means being true to yourself while adapting your message to your environment, maintaining your integrity while playing different roles in different situations.

As well as allowing a leader to be genuine, candor gives rise to another important quality: authenticity. In *True North: Discover Your Authentic Leadership*,[8] more than 125 leaders interviewed expressed a cohesive vision of this quality. Authentic leaders show a sense of purpose, establish long-term meaningful relationships, and spend time and energy on discovering their true self. As a result, they are more effective leaders. This line of research argues for continual search and testing of the self through real-life experience. It advocates reframing your personal story in order to understand who you are. Authentic leadership does not rely on a specific characterization of your leadership. Instead, it relies on a certain mind-set and willingness to understand and discover where your leadership can best serve and work for others. Achieving self-awareness is a never-ending process that falls out with the reach of existing standard assessment tools used to measure our intelligence or personality. The learning processes associated with the relational circuit I present later provide a more nuanced view of the complex and moving nature of the human beings that we are.

Self-Awareness, Humility, Honesty, and Resilience
Knowing and accepting ourselves as we are requires us to recognize that we are not perfect. Knowing that is one thing; what we do about it is another matter altogether. It is the power of humility: to make us act upon the recognition of our imperfection. Leaders, like parents, are often placed on a pedestal that contradicts the very idea of flaws and imperfections. For small children, a parent is like a god, an eternal presence that eases and soothes all troubles and fears. When a child discovers that his parents are real, live human beings, the world changes: suddenly, humanity has a different face and life is more dangerous and fragile. A leader has the same capacity to inspire images of greatness that mask the human inside the position. With humanity comes imperfection. How can we acknowledge and work on our imperfections?

I was lucky enough to grow up in a family that had sports in their blood. My grandfather taught me how to ski in 1965, when I was three years old, setting me on a path that saw me compete in several different sports and learn a lot about my imperfections on the way. Practicing flip turns in swimming, serves and volleys in tennis, or the slalom technique in skiing, I was constantly faced with my imperfections and the need to improve.

The rigor, discipline, and respect induced by the rules of sports provide great lessons in genuine self-awareness. Winning in sports is not so much about beating your opponent as winning control over yourself and your actions and reactions. When it comes to winning, talent is useful but not sufficient; respecting the rules and working hard are critical. Only with practice can you surpass your limits and improve. You also have to give

100 percent of yourself and be utterly and genuinely involved if you want to make significant progress. This ongoing process of self-questioning and self-improvement is a great source of enrichment that teaches you humility, as long as you are capable of learning from your failures and losses.

What type of loser are you? Think back to childhood when you were playing games or sports. What was your reaction when you lost? And how is this reflected in your relationship with failure in adult life? Being genuine means that we accept our mistakes and are capable of analyzing our failures and learning from them. The former CEO of Procter and Gamble (P&G), A. G. Lafley, speaks of his failures as a gift. In a 2011 interview in the *Harvard Business Review*,[9] Lafley explains how he learned from failed acquisitions. He analyzed the root causes of the failures and found that all of them were of a relational nature: the absence of a winning strategy, slow or inadequate integration, synergies that didn't materialize, cultures that weren't compatible, leadership that wouldn't play together in the same sandbox.

In 2005, P&G's failure rate for acquisitions stood at around 70 percent. Then it acquired Gillette. This was one of the group's ten biggest acquisitions ever; failure was not an option. Lafley used the knowledge and experience he had gained from analyzing previous failures to implement a new approach to acquisitions at P&G. He put in place a dedicated team and processes and focused on value creation and integration. A senior manager supervised every value creation initiative. Gillette's CEO was placed on P&G's board to facilitate value creation and acquisition integration alongside P&G's chief financial officer (CFO). They adopted an integration sequence whereby joint teams of leaders were involved in different aspects of integration: P&G's chief information officer (CIO) worked on the integration of information technology (IT); the chief procurement officer (CPO) and general manager took care of purchases; Bob McDonald, the current CEO, was in charge of integrating global operations. A red-yellow-green process was applied to track progress on every phase of the integration.

These tactics led to revenue synergies and joint product innovation. By objective criteria like cost synergies and revenues the merger was a great success, yet Lafley recognizes that some things could have been done better. He particularly highlights people development, acknowledging the company's failure to retain some key people and make optimal use of others. Helping people to grow and searching for the right place for each individual to thrive is not an easy task in a merger or acquisition. It is a task that often requires persistence and resilience.

Resilience is a capacity to pick yourself up after failures, learn from them, and apply the knowledge acquired from those experiences into new situations. Given that we are living in a complex, fast-moving, relational world, this is a never-ending process; business is full of setbacks that you must overcome and keep pushing through, and constant evolution and reinvention is required to thrive in a rapidly changing environment. Resilience is a key component of genuineness because it implies the capacity to dive inside yourself, acknowledge your failures and mistakes, and find the strength to stand on your own two feet with confidence.

I believe that sports are a great source of inspiration when it comes to finding and developing the genuine side of our sense-relational leadership characteristics. The world's greatest sporting champions are winners because they have the mental strength and confidence to accept small failures, like fluffing a simple forehand or missing a putt, and not let those failures distract them from their overall goal. In the same way, great leaders must find the resilience to maintain their trajectory and their vision whatever the frustrations, failures, and complexities of their daily professional reality.

Clara Gaymard, whom we met at the start of this chapter, will never forget the strongest, most resilient moment of her life. She was working in Egypt at the time. Her baby son fell sick and needed to be repatriated on medical grounds. There was a risk that he might die during the flight if he didn't have enough oxygen, so a specialized nurse was appointed to supervise him. At the airport in Cairo, however, it turned out that the nurse didn't have the necessary visa and couldn't travel to France.

Gaymard decided on the spot to send her two older children, who were just three and four years old, on to France, alone on the plane with strangers; she stayed behind with her sick baby and her two-year-old daughter to sort out the nurse's paperwork. In the taxi home from the airport the baby was fighting for breath because of the heat in the car, which was stuck in a traffic jam. Gaymard was desperate: her son was dying in her arms while her little girl sat next to her, looking on with worried eyes. Instead of panicking, she kept calm and asked the driver to take a side road so they could get moving and get some air. Her baby started breathing more normally again.

Because she felt her daughter's eyes upon her, Gaymard found the strength and resilience to surpass her inner impulse to break down and cry, which would have done nothing but transfer her own anguish to her child. "In my leadership role, the way I smile, the way I look at and listen to people, or react physically and emotionally in difficult moments, is a significant source of trust in my organization. I stand strong because I know people look up to me and expect me to hold on. Being strong in difficult times will breed trust from the people who work with me."[10]

Resilience is a measure of our ability to face difficulties, to pick ourselves up after failures, to make tough decisions and know that we will live with the consequences. Being resilient means accepting that we are not perfect. Once we do that, we can start working on strategies to improve ourselves. One strategy is to think of ourselves as incomplete. This is easy to see in team sports, where the different skills and physical abilities required to play different positions clearly show that individuals who are complete in some respects are incomplete in others: a quarterback could not play the role of the offensive guard and vice versa. An article in the *Harvard Business Review*, "In Praise of the Incomplete Leader," explains how leaders benefit from surrounding themselves with people who share their sense of purpose but compensate for their limitations or, simply, for their humanity.[11]

Henri de Castries, CEO of the Axa Group, one of the world's leading insurance and asset management groups with operations in fifty-seven countries, adopts this approach. As he explained to a group of MBA students at a conference in 2009, he is happy to recruit and quickly promote people who can do things better than he can because it makes the company thrive. An Indian MBA student walked up to him at the end of the talk to challenge that very statement by asking for a job interview. De Castries listened to him and was impressed by the student's genuine motivation and interest in the company. He gave him his business card and two weeks later the student had an interview; he was soon hired to be part of the business development team for Axa Assistance India.

The best leaders aren't just aware of their imperfections and incompleteness; they are not afraid of them. They are confident enough to rely on other people to play complementary roles. Sense-relational leaders surround themselves with people who complete their incompleteness. This healthy, humble approach is in contrast to the desire of many leaders to appear flawless, sometimes to the point of believing they are infallible, the expert in everything. Genuinely thinking you are at the top of the mountain, above the rules, above everyone else, the perfect being who knows better, is a dangerous game; the myth of perfection and omnipotence lies at the root of scandals or crises such as Enron and the failure of Lehman Brothers.

Job advertisements often betray this myth of perfection, seeking a sum of skills that no single individual could match. Recruiters seem to dream of perfect, exceptional individuals who will bring value at every level of their job and more. Few recruiters appear to understand the need for balance within teams so that everyone can find a place that is right for himself or herself while leaving room for others to find their places too. The fear of incompleteness in a dynamic and moving environment is similar to the fear of absence or loss: something is missing that only one thing or person can fill. In practice, filling the gap with some "imperfect" thing or person might alter the dynamic between the existing parts in such a way that the problem is resolved.

Incompleteness can be confused with failure or incapability if the need for cooperation and collaboration is not recognized. The desire to be genuine can result in a determination to do everything yourself. But no single individual can cover every task in a project alone; no one person should try to control everything or monopolize the floor. As such, delegation is a key aspect of leadership that is part of the savoir-relier mind-set.

The Risks of Being Genuine
There are, however, limits to the benefits of being direct, honest, and transparent. Paradoxically, being genuine can lead to behaviors that contradict the positive intentions attached to sincerity and goodwill. In our

relationships, for example, being genuine can cause us to be impulsive because we are too direct and want to share everything without reserve or self-control.

Knowing when to shut up is a way to protect yourself against this risk. You must learn to keep a "secret garden" that no one is allowed to enter. Sometimes it is better to hold back words and views that might negatively affect a situation or person simply because the timing is not right. Sometimes people are not ready to receive the information that your genuine self tells you to share. Effective communication involves providing the right type of information at the right time with the right structure and for the right purpose and audience. The choice of language, tone, structure, and content must be appropriate to the context and target. Using your senses to capture the different nuances of a situation and understand how they relate to each other and to yourself will equip you to make good decisions about what to say and what to hold back.

Being genuine without reservation can also induce naïveté and a lack of judgment. For example, once you really trust an employee, your genuine self will tend not to question that person's judgment and actions because you have a bias toward positive appreciation of his or her work. Loyalty and trust are fundamentally positive assets of the genuine leader, but when they are exercised without discretion and judgment they can blind him or her to reality. Genuineness in a relationship can lead to a refusal to see the downsides or mistakes that necessarily occur over time. The risk of being too genuine lies in a sheer openness that becomes a form of naïveté.

Being too genuine is just as dangerous as being too secretive. Introspection and awareness of the relational side of our being is the key to knowing where to draw the line. Holding back or not speaking one's mind does not prevent a person from being authentic or genuine. On the contrary, genuine leaders dare to be themselves and make their own decisions. They have built the self-awareness and confidence necessary to listen, exchange opinions, analyze, and then act decisively.

Now that we are aware of the risks and benefits of being genuine, we can concentrate on how to grow genuineness in sense-relational leadership.

The Challenge of Being Yourself

When I teach communication in executive seminars or MBA courses, I remind participants that communication is not a trick or a technique. It is a state of being. The toolbox approach to communication, which involves learning certain gestures to make a certain impact, will not take you very far. The advice I give my students is "Be yourself."

Though apparently simple, this advice has many implications. To be yourself, you first have to know who you are—and to know who you are is no simple task. You have to accept and live with the person you are, this strange animal that gesticulates, paces, shrugs, and gets nervous when it speaks in front of a crowd. Being genuine requires an awareness of the attitudes and behaviors that express what goes on inside you and who you truly are. They reflect your image and show your confidence or arrogance, your shyness or composure. Watching a video of a speech or presentation you have given to an audience and discussing it with a third party is the best way to become aware of your genuine self and the messages you are giving to the outside world.

But recognition is not enough. You need to act. In Chapter 4, I discuss the relational circuit, a savoir-relier toolkit for analyzing problems and developing solutions. However you approach the challenge of self-knowledge and self-perception, only with work and intensive practice will you learn to present your best, genuine self to those around you. Genuineness is the first step to building confidence, a confidence that acknowledges the value of incompleteness and the importance of coordinating and collaborating with others. The confidence acquired from being genuine opens the door to being our true selves and relating to others with empathy.

To sum up, being genuine involves a mix of authenticity, confidence, and humility that serve transparency and ease in communication, the capacity to truly be yourself while engaged in different tasks, roles, and situations. But the interpersonal skills that are so important for today's leadership in organizations require more than genuine behavior. Generosity is the second characteristic that is necessary for a savoir-relier leader. From focusing on you and yourself, let's turn to you and others.

BEING GENEROUS: BUILDING TRUST AND EFFECTIVE TEAMS

Pascal Cagni was the CEO of Apple EMEIA (Europe, Middle East, India, Asia) from 2002 to 2012. He is a dynamic, action-oriented man who puts passion and energy into everything he does. His relationships with others, both at home and at work, are engaged, dynamic, open, and never complacent. He likes to challenge and confront people.

This level of attention is not necessarily easy or pleasant for the people who are on the receiving end. His passion, engagement, and energy can be perceived as aggressive or intrusive at times, and the way he expresses himself does not always reflect what he truly thinks of a person. Nevertheless, I would argue that Cagni is a truly generous leader.

Commitment, Trust, and Attentiveness

Generosity is usually attached to a certain way of being. A generous person is usually seen as being driven by the desire to help others and do good for people. I would argue, however, that generosity is not an act driven by the intention to do good, but a characteristic that is built into every action that involves others. It is a reflection of how we see others and deal with others rather than a way of treating others. If you know when you are generous, then you are not really generous, because your generosity then has a purpose, an objective with an expected reward. Generosity does not expect return.

As Philippe Gaud, the Apple HR director who recruited Pascal Cagni in 2001, puts it: "Pascal can challenge members of his team in a meeting and put them 'on the grill,' giving them a very hard time, and then go for a drink with them when the meeting ends and have a great time. This form of engagement can be misunderstood, but Pascal does not look for recognition or any form of return. He does not want to please people or say what they want to hear. He does this at the risk of his own reputation and the impression people have of him. But he does it because he genuinely believes that he cannot be passive when he sees or hears someone who needs help, whatever form that may take. Pascal dedicates the same level of engagement when he's challenging a manager on the quality of a presentation as when he's collaborating on a humanitarian project."[12]

This form of generosity is genuine in that Pascal is giving his all. Whatever he's involved in is his only focus, the main priority. He becomes a coach who brings out the best in the people around him. He is the same person at work with employees and at home with his children. "He would manage his time to see his kids almost every night at dinner in spite of the heavy demands of his CEO position," says Gaud. "When I look at the growth of Apple EMEIA under his leadership and the four great kids he has helped to raise I can safely say he was effective in both roles. The interesting thing is that Pascal does not claim to be a coach, a facilitator, a parenting guide. In fact, he does not like these words very much. He does not want to be a coach or a facilitator but he is. Pascal never shows or underlines what he does for someone. He does it because this is the only way he can relate to others. He is genuinely generous."[13]

Moving from genuineness to generosity means moving from confidence to trust. Trust develops from the way you behave with your colleagues and employees. It is particularly important in difficult times when you need to stand strong in the face of adversity. As a leader, even if you are afraid, nervous, or agonizing over a complex problem, you must not transfer your own fears to others. As Clara Gaymard showed when she refused to panic in that Egyptian taxi, resilience is the resource that will give you the capacity to resist and contain your fears. Your personal life can teach you to build that resilience if you just dive and dig into your past and look for those moments when somehow you found the ability to stay strong and push forward.

Generosity, like genuineness, is a characteristic that is founded in perception, reliance, resilience, and responsibility. Good leaders are generous in the time and attention they give to members of their company. As we saw in the case of Pascal Cagni, generosity is about caring, sharing, and giving.

In their book *L'esprit du don* [The spirit of giving], Jacque Godbout and Alain Caillé describe the importance of the spirit of giving in our modern, liberal, and individualist society.[14] Giving creates interpersonal connections that strengthen and deepen the quality of relationships. To engage in savoir-relier implies endorsing genuine generosity as a source of giving. With a willingness to share and a desire to care, your leadership will find its expression in a place of exchange and respect across differences and boundaries.

Giving is more of an attitude than an act, and it does not necessarily require money. Indeed, generosity is commonly associated with money, as if it is the only thing that can be given. Incentives in the workplace are too often reduced to pay raises, bonuses, or other financial mechanisms to motivate and engage people. Many leaders develop reward systems that could be confused with generosity, but these rewards are mere mechanisms to stimulate short-term profits. This is not the generosity that sense-relational leadership promotes.

Recent research on motivation shows that fostering a shared sense of purpose, mastery, and autonomy in the workplace is far more effective in boosting performance than a financial incentive.[15] Sustainable growth comes with the trust built on cognitive and emotional generosity, on the development of a giving, sharing, and caring attitude. The genuinely generous person grows a mind-set that translates into much more than simply giving money. For example, the amount of time you give to a person will make a significant contribution to the quality of the relationship.

The gift of time is particularly important given our complex and ambivalent relationship with time, particularly when it comes to achieving a healthy work-life balance. Most of the executives age fifty to sixty with whom I have worked regret the lack of time they gave to their family, particularly their children. "I did not see them grow up," "I missed their best years," and "I was traveling so much that I wasn't there for them when they needed me" are phrases that come back time and again. Although people express regrets about not spending enough quality time with people, at home, or at work, when they are challenged on the reasons why, the answer is usually "Because I don't have the time."

Effective time management is, therefore, key to becoming a generous leader. In my experience, devoting a little quality time to one activity or person is far more efficient than spending a lot of time mixing many activities. Generosity is not a question of quantity but of quality. Generosity is what takes you from spending time with someone to spending quality time being fully engaged with them. Giving people positive attention builds their confidence and lets them know they can rely on you and trust you.

Personal attention is a powerful incentive and reward. When people feel good about themselves, they give their best to the job and are more successful. The spirit of giving is an asset as long as it is not reduced to money.

Collaboration, Caring, and Responsibility

Generosity implies the ability to engage with passion and energy, to give the best of yourself. Combined with genuineness, generosity opens the door to collaborative leadership, which empowers individuals so they can play their role effectively. No one can really empower another person; you can only create conditions that facilitate self-empowerment. Embedding the collaborative spirit of sharing in the structure of the organization is one way to create an environment of growth, movement, and engagement. A collaborative environment and a spirit of sharing create platforms for discussion and debate that leaders should encourage in order to open themselves to challenging and sometimes conflicting views.

In a collaborative working environment where relationships are built on trust, people get to know each other better and develop a stronger tolerance for individual differences. A generous attitude encourages greater openness to differences and a capacity to work with people from diverse origins and cultures. I saw this firsthand during the development of the HEC MBA program. Formerly a very "French" program with a fifty-fifty split of French/non-French participants, the HEC MBA is now an international program with more than fifty nationalities and 85 percent of students coming from countries other than France. The diverse academic backgrounds, professional experiences, and skill sets of these students have strengthened the program and fostered a spirit of collaboration.

To drive the benefits of that diversity still further, the MBA is now structured around core teams of five or six students. These teams are deliberately constructed to make them as diverse as possible in terms of nationality, academic background, professional experience, and gender. On the first day of the program, I would welcome the students as follows: "You are going to share your knowledge and experience in teams of people you don't know and haven't chosen to be with. This is a big part of your learning experience because you will have to depend on one another's expertise, ideas, and viewpoints in order to complete the numerous tasks required during the first year of your MBA. Of course, you don't have to love each other and you might even not like each other. But if you want to survive and get the full benefit of your investment, you must respect and care for one another."

This environment forces participants to adapt to other ways of working and thinking and obliges them to get along with different personalities. There are, of course, numerous conflicts, but these are an important part of the learning experience because in resolving these conflicts, the students learn about candor, trust, and tolerance and develop their self-awareness and humility. The "safe" environment of the MBA is a good place to learn that in the end, there is always someone who knows better or more about a given subject, and to understand the benefits of losing a battle if it means winning the war. Leadership roles vary with the subjects studied: an Indian engineer with seven years of experience in finance steps up to prepare a case study on financial markets; an entrepreneur who has run her family business in Brazil for five years takes the lead in a case on strategy. By obliging people from different backgrounds to work together toward shared goals that they have a vested interest in completing successfully, this system clearly demonstrates that diversity fosters adaptability and tolerance, both of which contribute to an effective collaborative working environment.

Relational coordination, particularly the hybrid form of relational bureaucracy developed by Jody Gittell and Anne Douglass, provides some of the most interesting insights into the value of caring in the business world.[16] Gittell and Douglass contrast the relational and bureaucratic forms of organization, acknowledging the strengths and weaknesses of each to come up with a relational bureaucracy model that combines the best of both. As they put it: "Role-based relationships of shared goals, shared knowledge, and mutual respect foster participants' attentiveness to the situation and to one another, enabling the caring, timely, and knowledgeable responses found in the relational form, along with the scalability, transferability, and sustainability found in the bureaucratic form. Through these role-based relationships, relational bureaucracy promotes universalistic norms of caring for particular others."[17]

Gittell and Douglass cite the example of Southwest Airlines, a company that has made the shift toward a mind-set of sharing and relationship building to increase productivity and improve well-being at work or, as they put it, "uphold a way of being that goes beyond any particular worker, customer or manager while being attentive to their particular needs. As a Southwest employee explained: 'There is a code for how you treat others here. The easiest way to get in trouble here is to break that code.'"[18] Relational bureaucracy supports knowledgeable and caring responses to others through the use of formal structures that embed reciprocal interrelating—both cognitive and emotional—into the roles of workers, customers, and managers.

This approach resonates with our examples of leadership: both Clara Gaymard and Pascal Cagni have established their own codes or values around sharing and genuine generosity and employ structures that encourage and facilitate engagement and care with sense-relationality. To the relational bureaucracy model and its cognitive/emotional dimensions of relationships, I would add the sensible or sensing dimension, which increases our capacity to build trust in a collaborative environment. The savoir-relier leader relies on his or her genuine generosity to build structures that encourage the use of our senses and sensibility as well as our knowledge and emotions. It is important to balance the notion of caring with the vigilance that all good leadership requires. The example of Pascal Cagni is a case in point. Caring does not mean accepting anything from anyone, including your boss. It means challenging people, testing limits, pushing talents, and watching for failures. Generosity and care come with attention or vigilance regarding others' imperfections. Good leadership comes with doubts.

To me, the epitome of generosity is the 1979 Nobel Peace Prize winner: Mother Teresa. She gave her life to the service of people and yet spent more than fifty years in doubt, as her correspondence revealed after she died. Doubt was her force, the energy that kept her serving the poor and traveling the world to help people. Doubt brings the recognition that we don't know it all, that there is always something to clarify and that the pursuit of self-awareness is an ongoing, lifelong process. This process keeps us moving and wanting to engage in relationships that will help bring a sense of purpose to our actions. Awareness of our imperfections and incompleteness can be a source of confidence when it is embedded in our capacity to be genuine. In the same way, doubt breeds the awareness that generosity can be subverted and abused by people who would take advantage of it. Doubt in the business environment enables us to challenge existing values and norms. Questioning is the only way to move forward, to "challenge the status quo," as Pascal Cagni liked to say to MBA students in his leadership talks. Questioning is also a way to open the door to different viewpoints and other perspectives on a problem.

The Risks of Being Generous

Being generous is often associated with being "soft," and it is true that generosity can hide a major flaw: excessive fragility or vulnerability. Devoting all your time and energy to a cause, person, or company carries the risk that you will lose your identity or self-esteem. Excessive commitment can lead people to forget their own health, to stop listening to what their body is telling them, to ignore the signs of fatigue that show they are giving too much. Generosity becomes vulnerability or fragility and can even lead to depression, when you spread yourself too thin and do not set limits.

Use your senses—primary senses, common sense, the sense of where you want to go, the direction you want to take—to develop a better sense of where to draw the line when you are about to do something you either don't believe in or simply don't want to do. In both your personal and your professional life, balance your generosity with a genuine focus on what is important to protect yourself from giving too much of yourself to others. In business, this implies keeping enough energy aside for nonwork activities to maintain a work-life balance.

The desire to please others is sometimes so strong that generous people will do anything for a person but hurt his or her feelings. In business, this can result in telling a person what he or she wants to hear instead of telling the truth. This behavior is the opposite of generosity; it becomes a form of hypocrisy or even manipulation and it does not serve business effectively. The whole field of consulting would greatly benefit from enhanced awareness of where that line should be drawn and from more balanced, genuine, and generous attitudes in its relationships with clients. When combined with a genuine attitude, generosity breeds trust, as the story of Pascal Cagni shows. But when pushed to an extreme, generosity highlights our vulnerability.

Expressing Generosity through Constructive Feedback
Savoir-relier leaders who struggle with an excess of generosity are well advised to develop their skills in constructive criticism. Giving feedback is a generous action that helps others to grow. By focusing on constructive criticism, we can help others while reducing our own vulnerability to some of the risks of being genuine and generous, such as becoming blind to flaws through an excess of trust or giving unearned praise simply to make the other person happy.

Giving feedback is a skill that can be developed in communication practice. The issue with effective feedback is one of honesty. One of my MIT Sloan students addressed the issue of honesty when giving feedback in his final self-assessment report for the core communication course of the MBA: "I mentioned to a teammate that I hoped my strong feedback regarding Jane had helped her rather than damaged our team cohesiveness. He said, 'I'm so glad you said that! We all felt the same way and she needed to hear it.' It felt good to know it wasn't just me but I realized that any other teammate could have given that feedback yet had chosen not to. Despite having the safest, most protected and supported feedback environment that any school could create, five of six teammates couldn't bring themselves to speak the honest truth to the seventh. If that fraction of smart, trained and motivated MBA students couldn't bring themselves to provide honest negative/constructive feedback, how much are we missing in our everyday interactions about what people really think?"

The experience of giving and receiving feedback in a constructive and honest way develops both resilience and humility. It is a great exercise to be practiced over and over. It enhances confidence and trust in our perception and judgment and that of the people around us. In business, 360° assessments are often used in personal-development seminars. When well managed, they offer a great opportunity to learn about yourself and can open the door to valuable exchanges and constructive criticism. Most

360° assessments take the form of a multiple-choice questionnaire built around the work setting and hierarchical relationships ($n + 1$, $n + 2$ peers, subordinates). The results of a 360° assessment are anchored in the relational dimension of the workplace rather than in the individual profile. The value of these assessments lies in their capacity to provoke reflection and self-awareness and in the discussions that follow.

In the early days of 360° feedback I was one of a group of twenty-five people from different organizations taking part in a leadership development program which offered a 360° assessment as an optional exercise. It required preparation and time from other members of the company, so only three participants decided to do it (I did not). One of them was handed her 360° report at the end of the training program and read it right away, but because the seminar had wrapped up, there was no time to discuss it with the other participants. She appeared to be totally depressed at the farewell lunch and didn't say a word even though she had been an active contributor during the seminar. I went over to her after we had finished eating. She confessed that she had agreed to do her 360° assessment because she thought the feedback would help her improve her work relationships. However, the feedback was so dry and severe that she could make no use of it. She felt hurt and demotivated; she did not understand why she was being attacked so harshly for things that seemed meaningless to her, like what she wore to work or the way she walked.

I wasn't from her company so I couldn't help her with the actual situation or the motives of the colleagues who had completed the questionnaire, but I engaged her in a conversation about the principle of the 360° assessment. I pointed out that the feedback had been taken in the context of the professional setting and the relationships involved. By going through the exercise of empathizing with those who had written the feedback and placing it in context, she started to put things in perspective and see what she had perceived as a personal attack in a new light. She suddenly became aware of moments and relational settings where there had been a lack of trust or she had behaved in a confrontational way. I advised her to analyze and understand how she was jeopardizing effective and trustworthy relationships through her personality and behavior and then go and talk about it directly to the people involved. She later told me how she had reached out to the colleagues who contributed to her 360° feedback and, as a result of those discussions, had increased her self-confidence and built trust. Even though it appeared that some of the feedback had been given in a negative or vindictive spirit, she found the generosity of spirit to accept that feedback and use it to build positive relationships that helped her and those around her.

For the sense-relational leader, generosity is an attitude, the second founding pillar of a savoir-relier mind-set. Generosity and genuineness together create the conditions for a generative mode of leadership that fosters action, creativity, innovation, and a strong shared sense of purpose.

BEING GENERATIVE: ENGENDERING COLLABORATION, INNOVATION, AND TRUST

To many, the story of Apollonia Poilâne will sound unreal. The CEO of France's premier bakery took on the leadership of the family business in 2002 when she was just eighteen years old, the day after her parents died in a helicopter accident. She had just been admitted to Harvard University. Rather than giving up either opportunity, she decided she would do both and successfully juggled her studies with running the company from her dorm room in Cambridge, Massachusetts, via the Internet, phone, and regular trips to Paris to meet with her staff. She had known from age sixteen that she wanted to continue the family tradition established by her grandfather and father; as she puts it, "The succession only happened sooner than it should have."[19] Today, the famous Poilâne loaf is more than ever the epitome of quality French bread, with fourteen tons produced daily at the factory in Bièvres and more than 6,000 loaves shipped every day to clients in more than twenty countries.

Innovation, Passion, and Creativity

Apollonia Poilâne is a true example of a generative, sense-relational leader born out of resilience. Being generative means being capable of production and reproduction, able to foster innovation and influence. It is a condition of effective leadership. The generative leader must do more than simply act; he or she must act with sense and passion, to drive progress, to innovate. Action for its own sake does not bring sustainable growth, but action that carries a sense of purpose and builds on genuine and generous mind-sets will foster the relationships that are necessary for innovation to flourish in uncertain times.

From a genuine and generous love for bread, Poilâne has driven a business where she is the "bread winner," generating quality and sense through both tradition and innovation. She has developed self-confidence from the example her parents set for her and from the resilience she grew out of her parents' death. It surprised people at the funeral when she stood up in front of more than a thousand people and read her speech without a tear, but I learned that her father had prepared her and her sister Athéna for the worst possible situation: "Because he was flying his helicopter and knew the danger, he had told my sister and me what we should do if the worst happened. We were prepared. In his will, he had written every step we should take and the people we could rely on." She was ready to build sense from her genuine enthusiasm for bread making and from the tradition she inherited from father and grandfather. "I knew what my responsibility was and I knew how to be self-reliant so I decided not to listen to those who tried to turn me away from my will. Now I want to transmit this passion to my sister's children, or my own, so the story continues to build sense for generations.[20]

A generative leader leverages his or her experiences of the world to build sense and identify opportunities, transforming them into concrete outputs: new ideas, new products, new strategies, or even new organizations. Innovation allows the leader to generate the future, to create the conditions for the future to emerge. Innovation is the means, at all levels of the organization, to translate the vision, the values, and the sense that the leader has articulated into tangible business outcomes. It becomes the vehicle that the leader uses to take his or her vision, ideas, and intuitions to market. In that sense, innovation is not an act but a mind-set that applies as much to products as to any other aspect of business operations.

To be innovative, the leader has to create a culture of resilience, agility, and processes that enable the organization to navigate through unknown waters to a new destination. Developing an environment for innovation to flourish is probably a leader's most difficult task. Designing and implementing business processes that will produce resilience while leaving room for agility requires a culture of risk and experimentation. The rules of the game need to ensure discipline while encouraging improvisation.

The productive tensions that are the essence of business performance find an interesting illustration with jazz. The success of a jazz band lies in its respect for certain essential rules and in trusting relationships that support improvisation and risk. Comparing jazz improvisation with product innovation, Ken Kamoche and Miguel Pina e Cunha developed a model of minimal structures that leave just enough space for solo performance and collaborative creation. The generative leader thrives by showing commitment and a high level of competence that inspires trust: "allowing an individual to determine the direction and flavor of the performance attests to the ensemble's trust in the soloist. The legitimacy of the soloist's 'authority' thus derives from their expert skill and ability to blend their competence with that of the other members."[21] In business, finding the right balance between structure and freedom—defining a set of social and technical structures that, paradoxically, create the freedom for innovation to take place—is one of the key challenges of the generative leader.

Freedom and Imagination

A dose of structure and another of flexibility also lead the way to creativity in education. As a professor for more than twenty-five years in France and the United States, I can testify to the opportunity to maneuver and create new courses out of expertise, interest, and research in a wider curriculum. The freedom to invent new pedagogical forms, to innovate with learning and content is often available even within the structure of a given department, program, or curriculum. Encouraging self-questioning and curiosity fosters the development of a generative mind-set, a critical eye, and a taste for experimentation.

Apollonia Poilâne's innovations are based on her sense of observation, her ability to connect different needs, and a genuine interest in doing good for people and for the environment. Her invention of a "spoon-cookie," offered to customers with their coffee, perfectly illustrates her genuine, generous, generative approach. She explains that when she was a little girl, she heard her mother telling her father how nice it would be to have a little cookie with the espresso coffee that the French usually drink at the end of good meal. Then, as now, coffee was usually drunk black with sugar. Today customers still order espressos, but the drink now often comes with a small chocolate or cookie that the customer can dunk in it to enjoy both flavors. And, of course, the coffee is also served with a teaspoon to stir the sugar. Poilâne's idea was to make little spoons using the recipe for the bakery's famous and delicious *sablés*, a type of shortbread cookie. The impact was immediate: it introduced new customers to the company's delicious sablé cookies, which are known as *punitions* by regulars at the bakery; it cut back on the need to wash hundreds of teaspoons every day; and it resulted in many customers ordering a second coffee just so they could enjoy another spoon-cookie. Poilâne's invention of the spoon-cookie was a genuine act, inspired by her love for her parents; a generous act, in that it makes an "unnecessary" gift of cookies to her customers; and a generative act, in that it has turned out to be good for business.

When I met with Apollonia Poilâne, I was struck by her drive, her passion, her sensibility, and her profound commitment to build sense from her experience. She speaks of bread as one would of birth or life, using words like *nurture* when talking of the nine months it takes to train a good baker. She tells the story of how her bread is made of four simple ingredients—sourdough, flour, water, and sea salt from the Guérande region—that generate a complex, subtle, and balanced loaf. She explains how bread sings and says that you must listen to it because it is not just about taste but also about its aesthetics. Under her leadership, business has risen to $18 million a year. She has opened two new bakeries in Paris and London and introduced new products. The company has 160 employees whom she respects and values for their genuine, generous love for their job and their professional passion for bread.

Poilâne has also carried out her father's interrupted journey by publishing his unfinished book, *Bread by Poilâne*, reaching out to society with a message about the power of quality and innovation associated with core values and a strong sense of purpose. And, on her late father's behalf, she asked the pope to erase *gourmandise*, which means a taste for sweets and is different from *gluttony* in English, from the seven cardinal sins. This gesture is a symbol of the value and the happiness that simple pleasures, such as eating Poilâne bread, bring to people. Her generosity and genuine attachment to family values were drivers that underpinned her resilience and sense of responsibility and turned her into the generative leader she is today, both for the family business and for society at large.

The Risks of Being Generative

Being generative can, however, lead to hyperactivity or action for action's sake. Being too generative may induce a lack of reasoning and loss of sense, as happens when research and development has no product definition at the end of the line, or finance focuses so heavily on profit that it loses sight of human or even legal dimensions. Senseless mechanisms such as those we have observed on the financial markets since 2007 are the result of people diving into action mindlessly, seeking performance without motive. Absurd spirals of algorithms and endless calculations to generate profits took down Lehman Brothers and allowed people like Bernard Madoff to generate massive frauds for years without being caught. The quest for short-term profits with the sole aim of winning often leads to the negative sides of the generative.

Referring again to sports, we observe the same phenomenon when athletes are willing to dope themselves to boost their performance and win at all costs without consideration for the rules or respect for other competitors. Whether pushed by their coaches and managers or simply driven by their own desire to win, these athletes lack the positive generative power required to draw the line and say no. Winning cannot be an end in itself. Without sense, winning for the sake of winning or performance for the sake of performance leads to fraud. There are limits to being generative that every talented person should acknowledge lest they negatively affect both the individual and society at large. The example of Lance Armstrong, the disgraced cyclist, and his team's doping conspiracy is a case in point. After being a hero in the world of cycling, winning seven Tour de France titles and inspiring a whole generation of young athletes, Armstrong is now known primarily as a cheat who pushed the limits way too far. He was generative, and perhaps even genuine and generous in his actions, but he certainly did not have the sense of purpose that comprises personal integrity and mindfulness for others.

The excessive behaviors shown by the Madoffs and Armstrongs of this world show the limits of a mind-set driven exclusively by short-term wins, profits, or performance. In our fast-paced and complex environment, the energy to create and produce must be balanced with respect for economic, environmental, and social rules. Let's now turn to the tools that can help foster a positive generative mind-set.

Developing the Courage to Build Sense
In our discussion of the genuine leader, we highlighted the importance of recognizing our imperfections. Imperfection, as explained by Ted Gioia[22] and Karl Weick,[23] is a way to look at a retrospective blueprint, use it to interpret your errors, and then move on with a new attempt. Such a mind-set turns errors into opportunities rather than failures. The ability to acknowledge an error and use it to move forward opens the door to improvisation, to taking risks and experimenting, whether alone or collectively. "Improvisation involves exploring, continual experimentation, tinkering with possibilities without knowing where one's queries will lead or how action will unfold."[24]

Like the soloist in a jazz band, we can find inspiration by experimenting and testing our capacity to generate new products that stem from creative ideas. Rely on your experience, perception, and competence and on the trust or reliance they inspire in yourself and in others. Accept that the process will result in some errors, wrong beats, or forced rhythms, and carry on until your idea generates results.

One specific technique I use to develop my students' capacity to be spontaneous, genuine, and generative is "impromptus." The exercise consists in pulling a random prompt out of a hat—examples include "You are an ant. Convince an anteater not to eat you," "Can a company be too big to fail?" and "What is true happiness?"—and instantly delivering a ninety-second speech in response. The student who is center stage doesn't have time to think and must act on the spur of the moment. The class listens and must guess what the prompt was. Participants tend to freeze when they read the prompt, but the game obliges them to concentrate and mobilize their mind and senses quickly. The spontaneity required to complete the exercise forces them to be generative; the feedback they receive on their performance gives them a better sense of how they performed in such a stressful moment of self-expression and helps them do better during the next impromptu session. The generative nature of the situation is seen in the energy required to put together a speech that is coherent.

Innovation is the first outcome of a generative mind-set that combines action and impact. An *MIT Sloan Management Review* article explores research that shows how companies need both "idea scouts" and "idea connectors" to generate open innovation.[25] The idea scouts seek out new technologies from around the world and provide new ideas, but translating these ideas into effective innovation requires idea connectors, also called innovation brokers, who have the savoir-relier skills necessary to connect the ideas into coherent and relevant concepts.

Marissa Mayer is an example of how idea connectors can play a crucial role. In her previous executive position at Google, Mayer played a central role in fast-tracking investment to new ideas by allowing all Google employees to pitch new ideas three times a week. She had the perceptiveness and confidence to select the best ideas and, importantly, recognized that this was a task that deserved her time and attention. She then leveraged her trusted position and her capacity to influence decisions and processes to champion selected ideas to Google founders Larry Page and Sergey Brin.

Mayer's role as idea connector at Google relates to all four principles of relationality: perception (as a natural flair for getting to know others), reliance (people trusted her), resilience (the courage to select and reject ideas based on her experience and accept that not all would be successful), and responsibility (seeking investment and seeing the idea carried out). She is, therefore, a good example of the new generation of savoir-relier leaders. She has the genuineness that gives her confidence in the selection process, the generosity to devote time and attention to others and their ideas, and the generative mind to pursue the innovation process for successful impact.

People who play a significant role in transforming ideas into innovative products are thus great examples of leaders. The important point to notice is that one does not need to be the CEO of an organization to be a savoir-relier leader. Sense-relational leadership is designed to foster leadership roles at many different levels of the organization and at different times. We are all but links in a chain that is connected to other chains. Our genuine, generous, and generative mind-sets are the engines that make those connections work harmoniously together.

3 SENSE AND COMPLEXITY
The Building Blocks of Savoir-Relier

With the overwhelming impact of rational and analytical thinking in global business practices, we have lost sight of the value and purpose of our senses. We take our senses for granted and neglect them to the point of becoming blind to the real world. But our senses play a major role in our capacity to apprehend the world. We need to reconnect with our senses and use them to reach out and connect people, ideas, experiences, cultures, and generations. Only by developing our own relationship to sense can we build sense for others.

The world of the senses is more ambivalent than the rational, analytical world. It is less reassuring because it is less controlled. The rational-minded person fears disorder, the unknown, the unexplained, and the inexplicable because life is easier to manage when everything has an explanation and can be reduced to an equation. Savoir-relier embraces this ambivalence and presents a new way to address complex decision-making processes by using sensory data as a key source of information that is complementary to our rational, intellectual capacities.

Although creativity, innovation, and discernment rely on other things than pure technical competence, that does not mean they are "soft," stupid, or inefficient. On the contrary, sensibility can increase our efficacy and effectiveness in action. Emotional intelligence and sensibility can improve leadership and decision-making processes. By giving sensibility its rightful place alongside rational, analytical leadership techniques and skills, we enhance our ability to understand and resolve uncertain and complex phenomena.

In order to transform your possible reluctance or suspicion regarding sensibility, we will analyze the many different meanings of the word *sense*. To demonstrate the value and power of sensibility and sensitivity, I will show that our senses are not irrational and unreliable but are, in fact, sources of valid and valuable information.

According to Webster's dictionary, the word *sense* has seven definitions:[1] meaning; the primary senses; conscious awareness/rationality; sensation; consensus; shrewd intelligence/common sense; and a specific direction. Each of these seven definitions has implications for leadership. For example, making better use of the primary senses can help develop relational leadership skills such as anticipation, intuition, and vision. A key strength of savoir-relier is its ability to embrace sense, in all its forms, and the rationality that has made the industrial era possible, giving rise to a form of structured flexibility that enables leaders to address the complex, unpredictable challenges of the twenty-first century.

SENSE AS MEANING

When the word *sense* is pronounced, what usually springs to mind is the idea of something that "makes sense." As Webster's dictionary puts it, sense is "a meaning conveyed or intended."

The Search for Sense

In today's world, younger generations are increasingly looking for sense, challenging their elders with their quest for meaning. Whether they are called "gen Z," "the net generation," "digital natives," "generation me," or even "the lost generation," one common observation is that they are in search of balance and sense. It is of the utmost importance for organizations today to understand that these young adults grew up in an environment built on social networks and immediate access to information. They believe they are entitled to work-life balance, are concerned about the planet, and seek meaning in what they do. This generation and the ones to come are multitaskers who can easily and instantly connect many different sources and sorts of data to get an answer or address a problem. The linear and rational processes of most organizations will struggle to integrate these young minds with their apparent lack of attention and focus. Organizations with socially co-constructed structures, where people develop interactions that are based on knowledge sharing, reciprocity, respect, and common goals, are likely to fare better.

Interestingly, though, this generation can display a remarkably blinkered understanding of sense and meaning. My students at MIT, a group of elite individuals from around the world, most of whom have a scientific or engineering background, provide an example. Educated to objectify problems and break them down into small pieces or units, they are masters at selecting and fragmenting information to decode it, separating and isolating elements in order to compute them. The computer scientists do this really well, reducing problems to the 0–1 binary mode of analysis. And it works. Scientific rigor gives us information about problems and enables us to find solutions to issues that were unsolvable. In my first session with a group of MIT students, when I told them we were going to work on sense and sensibility, they were clearly puzzled. As one of them said: "Our senses are not always reliable, which means they are suspect, so I don't rely on them." He later explained that he was wary and afraid of dealing with things that he couldn't control. However, learning to draw on sense and relying more on what our senses tell us about the world around us can increase our sense of control and leverage innate leadership capacities.

Sense Building vs. Sense Making

Analyzing the difference between sense making and sense building provides an easy first step into the world of sensibility for those of a rational, mathematical mind-set. Sense making, as explained by Karl Weick, is the process whereby people give meaning to experience.[2] It is a retrospective process that uses extracted cues or weak signals from past events to construct a storyline that makes sense in the present. In sense making, we see a transition from complex thinking to a relational process. Think of sense making as "a way station on the road to a consensually constructed, coordinated system of action."[3] The business books that we surveyed in

Chapter 1 identified key practices at successful companies and expected that replicating these practices would replicate success. The authors engaged in sense making, creating order from the past and present, only to discover that the future did not resemble the past.

Since sense making is systemic in nature, it can also be linked to the notion of an open system.[4] A central theme in both organizing and sense making is that people classify equivocal inputs in order to understand them, then project their interpretations back into the world to make it more orderly.[5] This notion also appears in the definition of relational leadership as "a pattern of reciprocal interrelating between workers and managers to make sense of the situation . . . to create a more integrated holistic understanding . . . triggering cognitive connections in the form of shared goals and shared knowledge."[6]

Sense building, on the other hand, contains a notion of construction and looks to the future. The process of building sense involves setting a goal and then working toward that goal by connecting the sources of knowledge, including sensory data, that are available to you. This process requires us to work on mastering sensibility, understanding our sensations, and learning how our senses will influence our behavior. Sense-builders are not afraid of relying on what their senses tell them about themselves because they have learned to use the information they get from credible sources effectively. This information is exactly like data gathered from a computer with two specificities: it is real and it is about you. To access and compute this information properly, you must be prepared to listen, look, touch, taste, and smell. The attention required here is active because the signals you receive will drive your behavior and your decision in a given direction to achieve a certain goal.

Why Sense Building Is Important

The following exercise will help you understand the difference between sense making and sense building. Bring to mind memories of the town or the house you grew up in and write as much as you can, as vividly as you can, about the place and the moments you experienced there. Now look around at where you live now and compare what you see and how you feel with the memories you put on paper. This comparative analysis is a sense-making exercise that helps you understand who you are and how you have been influenced by your life experience. The trace you leave on the page, your narrative, is something you can return to in order to gain a deeper understanding of who you are. Now project yourself into the future and write about your dream house or dream job; include as many details as you can about your surroundings and the people you see. Here, you are building sense for yourself and those you live and work with, or hope to live and work with.

I argue that leaders have a greater need for sense-building capacities than for sense-making capacities. Dealing with uncertainty and complexity requires an ability to turn to the future and create sense for others more than it requires an ability to make sense of our environment retrospectively. When building sense for an organization, the complex interactions between different entities must be carefully addressed in a coordinated and collaborative setting. The role and responsibility of the savoir-relier leader is to be mindful of the needs and actions of the group and of the individuals that compose it.[7]

THE PRIMARY SENSES

The second definition of sense relates to the primary senses: "the faculty of perceiving by means of sense organs . . . a specialized function or mechanism (as sight, hearing, smell, taste, or touch) by which an animal receives and responds to external or internal stimuli . . . the sensory mechanisms constituting a unit distinct from other functions (as movement or thought)." The reference to animals highlights the primal quality of our senses, that they are critical capacities that provided an evolutionary advantage. Our senses are captors of reality, a way to tap into data at the source. The information they provide is particularly revealing about our environment because it is not filtered by our analytical thinking.

Table 3.1 shows how each of the five primary senses, as well as the qualities of movement (kinesthetic) and balance (proprioception), affects our relational abilities and leadership skills.

Sensory information is transmitted directly to the brain, where it is interpreted in the context of our memories, emotions, and abstract thoughts. Focusing purely on sensory information requires an effort to push aside the

TABLE 3.1   The senses and their leadership impact

Sense	Organs	Act	Leadership quality	Relational skill	Dysfunction
Hearing	Ears	To listen	Understanding	Empathy	Deafness
Sight	Eyes	To look	Observation	Analysis/ vision	Blindness
Touch	Skin, fingers	To touch	Association	Contact	Numbness
Taste	Palate	To taste	Finesse/ discernment	Identity	Ageusia
Smell	Nose	To smell	Anticipation	Intuition	Anosmia
Kinesthesis	Eyes/legs	To move	Speed	Coordination	Paralysis
Equili-brioception	Inner ears	To stand and accelerate	Poise	Balance/ equilibrium	Loss of balance
Sensibility	Synapses	To perceive	Perception and relations	Sense-relational intelligence	Anesthesia

interference and interpretation of the mind, as it is difficult to be aware of sensory information without interpreting it. Given that our mind has the power to interfere with and manipulate external messages, exploiting our senses effectively requires awareness, attention, and patience. Furthermore, we must focus our attention on being present in the moment and receptive to the messages our brain is receiving. We must develop our ability to concentrate on external signals by tuning out internal interference as much as possible in order to avoid judgment, bias, and interpretation and let the information flow in from its source.

To help executives understand this concept and develop savoir-relier, I show them a painting and ask them to tell me what they see. Most mention what they think or how they feel about the painting. Learning to distinguish cognitive and emotional responses from purely sensorial input can be an incredible source of enrichment for leadership. It leads to the natural development of certain qualities, such as vision and empathy, that each of us has but tends not to exercise properly. This exercise also makes participants more aware of their tendency to spin incoming information according to their internal biases. Making a conscious effort to see more clearly helps us become more observant, which increases our capacity for vision; listening carefully enhances our ability to understand, which increases our ability to empathize.

The primary senses are not always reliable but they do always tell you something about yourself, and that information has a value in its own right. Learning to absorb and decode this information helps leaders find their footing in unexpected situations and have greater confidence in their intuition. Greater awareness, presence, and vigilance make us better able to measure, analyze, anticipate, and make sound decisions. Mastering our senses and allowing them to guide us will enable us to work with the tensions and contradictions that inhabit us and the world to take effective action and build a more "sensible" organization.

Hearing Can Lead to Understanding and Empathy
Knowing how to listen is the first step toward building a relationship with the other. In the animal world, sound is a vital channel for delivering information, signaling danger, and establishing communication. Whales, for example, "sing" songs of incredible complexity that enable them to transmit information to each other over huge distances—in some cases as much as two hundred kilometers.[8] Birds are another example, using songs to mark territory or attract a mate.

With human beings, however, absorbing information from sounds is not as straightforward. We establish our first contact with the external world through sounds heard in utero—our mother's voice, music playing in the room where she is—but once we enter the world, our minds start to interfere with the message nature is delivering. Most studies in communication show that it is virtually impossible to disconnect our thoughts from what we hear, that there is always interpretation of the other's message.[9]

Even so, our ears are a great source for gathering data that then affect our behavior. Listening provides information that goes beyond the meaning of words. The tone and intonation of a voice, its pitch, and vibrations express the sense beyond the actual message. At this level, hearing coupled with the capacity to concentrate on what the other person is saying leads to understanding: the ability to capture what a person is expressing rather than what we want to hear.

Listening is one of the most valuable leadership skills. A leader who listens is one step down the road to inspiring, influencing, and engaging the members of his or her organization; those who don't can quickly find themselves surrounded by people who are alienated or demotivated.

Here is a simple exercise to test your current listening capacity. Close your eyes, wherever you are, and spend three minutes concentrating on all the sounds you can hear, disconnecting them one from the other. You will realize that there are a multitude of sounds in your environment that you totally ignore in your daily activity. Once you have identified five specific, distinctive, and recurring sounds, open your eyes and write down what they are, placing them in three categories: annoying, neutral, and pleasant. You can then work on isolating those sounds, focusing on those that are pleasant and tuning out those that are annoying. Isolating and working on your capacity to listen is a way to grow your attention and respect for that which is outside you.

Effective listening and understanding make an important contribution to empathy, which is a critical skill in its own right. Empathy is the ability to be open and unprejudiced toward others by limiting the interpretation of words filtered by your own mind in order to reduce interference from your own personal bias and judgment. Addressing personal matters in conversation is a good way to work on interpretation and interferences and to concentrate on someone else's speech. Techniques such as rephrasing and prompting are good ways to develop empathy. But beyond the toolbox approach, the work that will most improve your capacity for empathy is genuine and thorough introspection on what it means to be "the other."

Sight Can Lead to Analysis through Observation

To understand the dominance of sight over the other senses, it helps to experience the world of the blind. There is a restaurant in Paris called Dans le Noir (In the Dark) where customers eat in the pitch dark. The serving staff, who are all blind, are there to help, but even so you rapidly realize the importance of things you usually take for granted: seeing your surroundings as you walk, the position of your cutlery and crockery—even apparently easy tasks such as putting food into your mouth are complicated. Smell and taste come to the fore as you try to guess what food you are eating, and the sounds in the room become much louder as you become more sensitive to movements and noises. You leave the restaurant with a heightened awareness of your surroundings, determined to make greater use of your senses in your daily life.

Our eyes give us access to direct and tangible information and drive the way we capture and interact with our environment. Sight is our main source of data; our eyes are lenses that mirror reality and show us the complexity of the world around us. Once we know how to translate or interpret what our eyes are seeing, sight becomes our most reliable analytical tool. Thus the clichéd expression, "I'll believe it when I see it."

The leadership skill attached to sight is observation, the capacity to identify the relevant information in a scene, a document, a person, or an object. Effective observation requires "intensity of attention," which is described by Warren Bennis as one of the most prominently valuable leadership skills because it has the potential to generate discernment and better judgment.[10] With awareness and attention you discover the limits and the value of distinct observation and discernment; by exercising patience, you can then develop the associated relational skill, the capacity for analysis and vision.

Analytical skills in savoir-relier leadership can be compared to those developed by airplane pilots, who can analyze and connect multiple sources of information in a matter of seconds. Many of the sources come through the eyes, which have to select, detect, and manage large amounts of data, sometimes from diverging or even conflicting inputs or signals, in order to analyze them to make a decision. In the modern world we are subjected to an overwhelming volume of visual data, be it on TV screens, billboards, smartphones, or tablets, all of which has to be filtered by the eyes and the brain. Savoir-relier helps us not only to connect and analyze those external visual inputs, but also to be conscious of the subjectivity of our perception and interpretation of that data. We rely on a combination of subjective perception and objective detection, a mix of intuition coming from experience and analysis coming from observation.

The leadership skills attached to the next three senses—touch, taste and smell—are not as obvious. They do, however, have important leadership implications.

Touch Develops Association and Sensation

Touch is sense in its purest form; it is at the heart of relationship building. Often suggestive and sensual, touch is the primary source of contact for animals and human beings.

Let me share an incredible example of the power of touch. *Haptonomy* is a method used to establish sensible and emotional contact between parents and their baby.[11] The father and mother use touch to build a physical relationship and establish a dialogue with their unborn baby by caressing the mother's abdomen in a specific way. This establishes communication as the fetus responds and moves inside the womb toward the hand. Sometimes contact is initiated by the fetus: when hands are placed on different parts of the stomach, the baby moves to establish contact, so the relationship can begin as it would in the form of dialogue. Babies who have experienced haptonomy as a fetus have been shown to be unusually and consistently tonic and outgoing after birth. Haptonomy is touch used as a source of openness and contact between an outer and an inner world.

Touch translates to the leadership skills of contact and association. It relates to our networks, a major subject of research today.[12] Through contact, we build correspondences with other senses or across other elements. We use the expression "to be in touch" or "out of touch." A person who is "out of touch with reality" often shows no sensation or feelings for others and is isolated and closed in; he or she shuts down from the world and cannot accept interactions with others. In addition to these conceptual uses of touch, there are physical reminders that the skin is itself an extraordinary medium for contact and an expression of deep inner sensations. It delivers information about our inner being through allergies, for instance, where eczema, spots, and itching are the external evidence of something going on inside.

The relational skill attached to touch is the capacity for contact. *Touching* and *feeling* are often used interchangeably, a misconception that confuses the physical sense with the emotional state. With touch as the cognitive skill, a person can indeed grow a capacity to detect people's sensibility through contact. Touch carries a cultural dimension too. People from Latin cultures, for example, are often perceived as warm and open because they come from a culture where people touch one another more easily and kiss in greeting. Nordic or Asian cultures, on the other hand, tend to be perceived as reserved and formal because they maintain a greater physical distance from one another.

Taste Is Linked to Finesse and Identity

Applied to leadership, *taste* takes on the figurative meaning of "having good taste." Good taste and an appreciation for beauty often go hand in hand. The capacity to distinguish and identify beauty through colors, shapes, light, and atmosphere, or pitch, rhythm, and harmony, is related to a distinctive leadership skill: finesse. Finesse is important in a leadership role as, in addition to being a sign of culture and education, it contributes to discernment or judgment.

Finesse is also a capacity for nuance and cultural sensibility. The quality of a person's conversation and exchange and their sensitivity and attention to different cultures can have a tremendous impact on their business relationships with clients or partners. When tough decisions have to be communicated or executed, sensitivity to the audience's cultural expectations may affect the future of the organization. There are many ways to develop taste and finesse, most of which are fun and educational: going to a museum and taking the time to look at famous works of art to understand beauty; attending a wine seminar and learning to taste the different wines to recognize the flavors and identify the age and origins of the grapes; participating in a cooking seminar. All of these activities will help you appreciate and develop this sense and learn to exercise it more.

As a relational skill, taste is relevant to the personal and subjective nature of things and leads to the notion of identity: this wine is unique for its specific taste of raspberry and myrtle; that institution has a unique identity represented by a logo and signature that convey its core values. For example, Pernod-Ricard, the French wine and spirits company, uses the signature *créateurs de convivialité*. Each of the brands within the company has its own identity, but this shared tagline provides them with a common culture. Company taglines can provide an interesting insight into the notion of corporate identity and the coherence and harmony of a business as it evolves over time.

At a figurative level, the French expression *chacun son goût* (equivalent to the English expression "each to their own" but literally meaning "everyone has his own tastes") testifies that taste is associated with individual rights: "It is my right to prefer this melody, this painting, or this person over that one." Hence taste reveals the value and force of subjectivity in our relationship with the world around us. As the supporting sense for our subjectivity and singularity, taste can be seen as the founding sense of our identity: it is both singular and shareable, both individual and social. Taste is also often combined with and complementary to smell, the last of our five primary senses.

Smell Is Linked to Intuition

From fine perfumes to unpleasant odors, scents affect our perception of the environment. Odor perception is a complex process that involves the central nervous system and can evoke powerful emotions and memories as the olfactory signal reaches the amygdala, which participates in the emotional processing of sensory data. Odors can affect our concentration or our feelings about a person, place, food, or product. People carry smells in their skin that characterize them and that are more agreeable to some than to others.[13]

As well as being a source of relationship building at a very primary level, smell is linked to instinct and intuition. We say we "smell a rat" when we know something is amiss but cannot put our finger on it. The French term *avoir du flaire* is used to refer both to dogs that are able to track a scent or sniff out truffles and to people who have a talent for predicting and anticipating events. Isolating the sense of smell and making it responsible for intuition is, of course, not the point here. Instead my aim is to highlight the link between the subtle, often imperceptible, sensory clues that allow us to "smell" something intangible like danger, and the value of intuition, which is too often disregarded by rational minds. Leaders and organizations that rely on intuition do not use smell as their source, but they do understand that intuition has a basis in reality and is derived from the information we absorb from the world around us. As we will see, the ability to trust these first impressions and intuitive perceptions is a defining characteristic of the savoir-relier leader.

The Relationship between the Senses and the Emotions

To wrap up the discussions of the first two definitions of sense—"meaning" and the "primary senses"—here is a final exercise that I use in my relational leadership class. Students are asked to choose an object that is tied to a meaningful moment or person in their life and that also awakens one of the five primary senses. They bring it to class and tell the story of the object and the sensory memories it evokes for them.

The emphasis on sense—both the meaning of the object and the senses used to perceive it—creates a moment of awakening where sensibility brings out the depth and genuine expression of each individual. This exercise is also a way to build an atmosphere of trust and respect within the class and can be replicated in different settings and formats. In my twenty-five years of teaching and training around the world, I have always experienced strong positive moments with this session, genuine moments of awareness, sharing, consensus, and drive, which are other ways to address and build sense for the people involved.

SENSE AND RATIONAL, OBJECTIVE THOUGHT

Sense as Conscious Awareness: Promoting Rationality through Sense

Let us consider how sense connects sensibility to rationality and provides a new perspective on rational thinking. The senses, as we have seen, deliver information to our brain and provide us with an awareness of reality as it stands.

However, our brain interferes with the data we receive by drawing inferences based on existing information and memories. We interpret our surroundings, transforming observable external data into filtered data that reflects our existing beliefs. We make assumptions about the data we receive based on what we already know and believe, and then we draw conclusions that incorporate those assumptions. We use those conclusions to update our understanding and beliefs about the world, and so the cycle begins again.

This process is extremely helpful in some cases—as when Régis was able to save me and my friends from the avalanche because his brain interpreted incoming data in the context of his past experiences on the mountain—but it also accounts for the bad judgments we sometimes make when we jump to conclusions without making a conscious effort to consider the real world as it is or people as they are. We can reduce this negative interference by paying closer attention to what source data is telling us and reining in our natural tendency to rely on subjective interpretation.

Whether you call it perspective or point of view, subjectivity is an integral element in the kinds of nonmathematical analysis that leaders undertake daily. Moreover, objective knowledge presupposes clear vision, which necessarily requires an understanding of our connection to the world. Recognizing and being fully conscious of our own subjectivity is, therefore, a major step in addressing relationships and understanding of the world around us. Acknowledging and accepting our subjectivity is far more productive than fearing and denying it.

Chris Argyris uses the term "ladder of inference" (see Figure 3.1) to describe the self-perpetuating process whereby our existing beliefs affect our interpretation of new data, which leads to biased conclusions, which

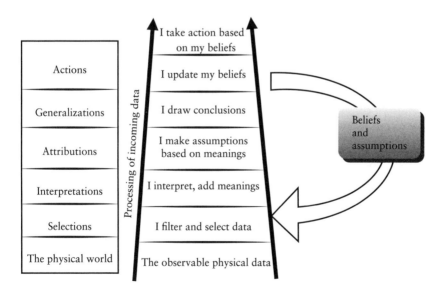

FIGURE 3.1   Ladder of inference

become new beliefs that affect our interpretation of new data. Once we are aware of this process we can start to consciously question our assumptions and challenge our conclusions with contrary data and opposing views. Acute perception combined with a conscious awareness of the reality around us hence becomes a source of rationality. Using conscious awareness helps us make better, more balanced judgments; establish more reliable appreciations of situations; and take more suitable and effective actions.

The following dialogue over a competitive relationship illustrates this point. John is seeking advice from his colleague, Kate, about his plans to apply for a managerial position that just opened in their division. He assumes Kate isn't interested in applying. Kate thinks John does not have has the skills to become a manager. Furthermore, unbeknownst to John, she intends to apply for the job herself. In the conversation, both are totally "up their ladder" (as per the ladder of inference in Figure 3.1) and totally unaware of each other's reality. The resulting conflict is inevitable:

John (confidently): "This job is for me. I have so many ideas about where our division should go, and I definitely deserve a leadership role. What do you think, Kate?"

Kate (thinking he is out of his mind but remaining cautious): "Well, you've been here longer than any of us, and you certainly know a lot about the job. But are you sure people on the team are ready to work for you?"

John (irritated by Kate's lack of enthusiasm but firm in his mind): "I think I'm pretty good at respecting people and encouraging sharing and collaboration. And I know I can shake things up and generate bigger profits."

Kate (annoyed by John's lack of awareness): "Yes, but it's always difficult to have a colleague become a superior. You won't be one of the boys anymore; you'll have to tell people when they're wrong instead of being the easygoing one all the time. How are you going to handle that part?"

John (refusing to hear Kate's point, becoming increasingly irritated by her implied criticism of his performance): "I get on well with everyone on the team—I'm sure they'll follow me. Wouldn't you?"

Kate (thinking it is out of the question and annoyed that he doesn't see her as a potential candidate, closes the discussion): "I think it's more complicated than you realize . . ."

Neither John nor Kate benefits from the discussion or learns from the other's viewpoint because each person is way up their ladder, holding back relevant information and anchored in their own beliefs about the job opening. As a result, conscious awareness of the context is literally impossible. To improve a situation like this one would entail work on inquiry and advocacy. Inquiry involves capturing information, data, and ideas from another person. Advocacy is speaking in favor of or defending someone or something—for example, to persuade people on your team to share your point of view. These are two key principles in effective dialogue and two aspects of sensibility that allow people to come down their ladder and build genuine or straight talk.[14]

When you try to convince others of your viewpoint, make sure you take account of their viewpoint and perspective. As we saw in our discussion of the generous leader, the idea is not to speak your mind without reserve and say everything you are thinking. Rather, enable the conversation to progress by opening up your mind and clarifying where you really stand. In the dialogue between John and Kate, if Kate had simply stated: "You know, I'm not as senior as you are, but I have proven management skills from my previous job and am also thinking of applying for the post. It seems likely to me, however, that the company might want to recruit outside to avoid tensions," then the dialogue would have been much more productive. Instead, Kate implied that she had doubts about John's ability to lead the group while John blindly assumed that Kate would support him because she had been a team player since she joined the company.

Inference gets in the way of conscious awareness. It can prevent people from speaking honestly and responding appropriately to verbal and nonverbal cues. Use the ladder of inference regularly as a way to remind yourself and others about where they truly stand when engaging in a relational situation. A simple comment like "Come down your ladder and hear what I am saying" or "Look at this fact or data for what it is" can be enough to bring conscious awareness and informed decisions back to the fore and improve working relationships along the way.

This approach to rationality shows another value of sense as a reliable source of analysis. It can help us understand complex problems and be better prepared to make relevant, sustainable, coherent decisions. Our capacity for judgment is an indication of the quality of our internal processing loop that takes incoming information and existing beliefs and filters them to confirm our ideas and analysis.

Sense as Intuition: Learning to Trust Your Instincts
Our fourth definition of sense relates to sensation, which is closely related to intuition. As we noted earlier in our discussion of smell, and the ability to "smell a rat," intuition is a key relational skill that is often misused or misinterpreted.

I enjoyed many years of downhill ski racing in my youth, but in adulthood my life and career had kept me away from the slopes. Encouraged by my children to compete again, I decided at age forty-one that I would try to win a national-level ski championship. But I had stopped racing at age twenty and the technique had changed radically in the meantime. In the 1980s, slalom poles were made of stiff wood and the goal was to trace the fastest possible route between the poles without hitting any of them. The slalom skis were relatively long and thin with large blades to hold on to the ice as the skier moved swiftly from one ski to the other. Today, slalom poles are made of flexible carbon, which means they bounce when the skier hits them with his or her fists and legs. The skier's feet must be wide apart and move in parallel on short, thick skis that maintain good contact with the ice and snow. I had a lot to learn if I was going to be competitive again.

Learning required agility and adaptation. I had to get rid of automatic behaviors that were inscribed in my subconscious and my muscles and consciously, deliberately, learn new sensations and develop new reactions that fitted with the new situation. Building new sensations requires the capacity to step outside our existing habits and behaviors and look for new sensory landmarks. Letting go of old habits and starting over is a way to rediscover yourself and research this "who" inside you that is constantly moving and changing. As we will continue to see, reflexivity and introspection are instrumental in relational leadership and developing savoir-relier. Relearning to ski challenged my capacity to respond with agility by listening to the signals my body was sending me. Paying conscious attention to those signals enabled me to develop new skills, adapt to a new context, and perform in a new environment. This kind of work on the inner self, the subjective sensible self, is a great opportunity to build sense by reaching a balance with the rational, objective world.

Let's now shift from these individual perspectives on sense and see how leaders can leverage their own sensibility into the realm of collective awareness and the collective use of sense.

Sense as Consensus: Making Solidarity a Leadership Asset

Consensus is a position agreed upon by a group as a whole. It is the process used to generate widespread agreement. The power of the word *sense* resides in its ability to capture both collective and individual dimensions. The multiple meanings of the word *sense* account for the power of savoir-relier—sense leadership—in addressing both individual and organizational issues. Consensus is a necessary stage in team management and product development. Consensus during the process is a source of performance.

Consensus brings us to the notion of solidarity, as seen in dramatic events like 9/11 or Fukushima, where people spontaneously came together with a common purpose to tackle a problem. Drawing lessons from such examples, we can see that motivating a group and building the common understanding that underlies collective agreement is a critical part of effective leadership. When leaders fail to construct this common understanding, the outcome can be deeply negative.

Karl Weick describes the case of a competent team of sixteen firefighters who were sent to fight a minor wildfire sparked by a lightning storm.[15] The gathered team was rather inexperienced and the team leader hadn't had much time to get to know the individual members. But the mission was clear and simple and they anticipated extinguishing the fire within twenty-four hours. However, the fire suddenly and unexpectedly switched and headed toward the team. In a matter of minutes, what should have been a routine mission turned into a nightmare. The leader was confronted with an unexpected situation and made counterintuitive, creative decisions to get his team out alive. He set a new fire on the only escape route, then asked the team to drop their tools and lie down on the ashes where he had set the fire. The team, not understanding the thinking behind his orders, did not obey him. They disengaged, each running away in their own direction to save their own life. Thirteen people eventually died in this tragic event; only the leader and two members of the team survived. The lack of sense making and consensus led to dispersion and chaos.

It takes constant effort and savoir-relier skills to create consensus. The next definition of sense, common sense, relates to another leadership skill that is too often overlooked.

Sense as "Common Sense": Using Judgment with
Relational Intelligence
Common sense is the positive flip side of the "ladder of inference" discussed earlier; it is our ability to use existing knowledge and beliefs to interpret information and draw conclusions that reflect both reality *and* experience. Our analytical mind often obstructs the obvious answers provided by common sense. Although mathematics and science give us the ability to break problems and situations down into equations and numbers, they can also tempt us to try to explain every phenomenon by analytical judgment. Focusing too heavily on details can cause us to lose our sense of the whole.

Common sense is the capacity to look at the world as it is rather than as it should be, might be, or could be. One summer I took part in a family event where we had tests to take and enigmas to solve in different places along the coast of the beautiful French island of Corsica. In one place we had to obtain a precise reading of the depth of the sea. A friend, the captain of the boat we were on, jumped into the water to take the measurement with his brand-new, high-tech depth meter. A few seconds later he was standing in the water, proudly reporting to his wife: "Nine and a half feet." She was diligently writing the answer on the quiz sheet when one of the kids, who was only eleven years old, said, "But that's not possible. Dad is standing and he isn't nine and a half feet tall!" The child's common sense resonated against our adult minds, which had abdicated their responsibility for thinking in favor of blind faith in supposedly reliable tools.

A critical mind and an acute awareness of the signals the world gives us are also ways to nurture our common sense. For example, when a person works in cross-cultural settings, knowledge of individual cultures is important to address a group or team. This knowledge, however, must be tempered by observations of how individual people *actually* behave. In today's world, where many people have an international education or have family or social ties to a range of cultures, it is of the utmost importance to balance one's appreciation of cultural differences with respect for the individual and the messages they communicate through their behavior. Common sense reminds us to be aware, attentive, and vigilant and to be patient enough to truly apprehend a situation.

Sense as Direction: Developing Vision from Sensory Data
The seventh and final definition of the word *sense*—a direction—also represents a universally recognized skill in leadership. Clear direction gives people something to focus on and push toward, a common set of goals and values that mobilizes their energy. Although it provides a sense of purpose, it is something that many companies have lost.

Indeed, while the notion of vision is central to every organization, it has often become nothing more than a mechanical exercise executives go through in order to exist. A company must have a "vision and mission." The vision is based on values, and the mission is translated into a "mission statement," which is supposed to drive the strategy that people will execute. But this vision-mission exercise has too often become just that: an exercise. Deprived of its original anchor in sense, the vision usually lacks genuine meaning. More often than not, the descriptions of visions and mission statements on company websites are totally interchangeable between organizations: they use the same words, refer to the same values, employ buzzwords like "corporate social responsibility" and "community" to tick the boxes of what good or great companies must do and must be. The notion of identity, the sense behind the vision, is absent.

Leaders must define a sense of purpose that carries meaning for the organization and the people who contribute to its growth. This sense of purpose is like a guide who takes a group of people on an expedition across complex and difficult paths. It must be embodied by the leaders embarking on the trail and by the people who follow along with them. The expedition will succeed if the relationships that are built between the members of the group are strong, trustworthy, and focused on a shared goal, in spite of and thanks to the changes and differences embodied by each member. The vision is the shared direction that people are moving toward.

Whether you are crossing the desert or trying to enter a new market, it is not the final objective that matters the most but the path that you are taking to get there, the people you are going with, and the reason you have—both individually and as a team—chosen that goal. Each individual comes with his or her own perspective and experience. Rather than allowing that to pull you in different directions, use consensus, common sense, and sensibility to construct a dynamic process that makes the most of those individual differences.

This last definition of the word *sense*—the direction, vision, and sense of purpose of the organization—reminds us that leadership, even with an idea of shared or distributed practice, needs a driver, a guide.

Sense as a Means to Open Our Minds
A savoir-relier approach restores the value of our senses as a cognitive function that gives direct knowledge and data. Sensing delivers information at its source and connects us to the real world of touch, sight, and hearing. When leaders are capable of assimilating all of their sources of knowledge, the quality of their understanding of situations and events is much more acute. We are better able to combine knowledge and experience when we are more alert and mindful.

Our senses are a decisive factor in the way we manage and make decisions. With a greater awareness of our senses and the data they provide, we can translate our experiences, our appreciation of the environment, our confidence, and our courage into effective action. Savoir-relier trains leaders to perform this translation, transforming sensibility and sensitivity into a source of confidence for taking action in difficult and complex situations.

In my own leadership experience, I constantly struggled with the question of where I should be. I knew I was in the driver's seat and that my role included inspiring and engaging others. But I also needed to step back, observe, and listen. Instead, I was in the light all the time. The way I behaved, or simply the way I was, who I was, had an impact on our business. I was delivering speeches to large audiences; responding to the media; convincing corporate leaders to support us; pushing and pulling students, faculty, staff, and various partners; setting the way forward. But I often wished I could just sit back and watch for a while. And I could not. I was expected, needed, demanded in the front seat, behind the wheel. This was where my responsibility lay. But one should know that stepping back is part of leadership, that leaving room for time and sensibility to set in will make a difference.

I was forced to do that at one point in my leadership for personal health reasons. For six months, I had to step away from the day-to-day business. This period away opened my senses to the business and facilitated the path to success afterward. I was able to see better, to listen better. I remained in close touch with a couple of members of the organization and was kept informed about what was going on. The program was running just fine and I was pleased to notice that I was not so central after all, that the structure was in place and people knew how to make things happen—to a certain point.

Once in a Q&A session with the students and staff from the MBA program, I was asked a classic question—but I was not prepared: "What keeps you awake at night?" Even though it was a classic, I hadn't prepared an answer and took a few seconds to think. My response was: "I want the HEC MBA to perform thanks to you, not me. My dream is to see it run even better once I am gone, because I am just passing by while you students, you will always be HEC MBAs." I had learned to let go and understood that to lead effectively means making an impact, possibly a lasting impact by improving the way people feel and live, making people feel better, see better, listen to each other better. But to lead also means planting seeds, passing by and letting people grow as they should. It is like raising children. There is no recipe to educate your child because you, your child, and the environment in which you live are absolutely unique.

All the books, journals, and articles that are written to tell parents how to educate their kids are just there to reassure them that others have been there before, struggling with the same haunting question: "Am I a good mother?" "Am I a good father?"—the same type of question that haunts most good willing leaders. But there is no one way to raise a child. It is your senses and your sensibility that will drive you the best. And it is the same for leadership.

4   B U I L D I N G   S E N S E   B Y   E M B R A C I N G   C O M P L E X I T Y

A Core Capacity

Alcatel was founded in 1898. By 1993, it was the second-largest company in France by market capitalization and was a leading architect of internet communications solutions. It focused on connecting people and facilitating relationships through an offering of services and solutions that included end-to-end networks, cell phones, Internet equipment, and high-speed telecom. Between 1995 and 2006, the company increased its presence in the global mobile and fixed phone markets, with a focus on mobile telephone manufacturing. Alcatel became the third-largest producer of mobile telephone handsets in Europe, behind Nokia and Sony Ericsson, and became a global leader in DSL equipment, competing with U.S. companies such as Cisco and Lucent.

Lucent was part of the AT&T Technologies group until 1996, when it was broken off to compete more effectively with other telecommunications providers. Although its stock was highly valued and it had moved into new areas, like telephone switching, optical, data, and wireless networking, the split from AT&T had left Lucent in search of an identity and a sense of purpose. On April 2, 2006, Lucent announced a $13.4 billion merger agreement with Alcatel, which was 1.5 times its size, to create a Franco-American telecommunications equipment manufacturer with revenues of $25 billion. The merged company was to become the leader in its sector with the same initial purpose of connecting people and facilitating relationships—this time around the globe. This was the first merger of a major U.S.-based networking hardware company with a non-American company. It was meant to respond effectively to the increased competition faced by the Western telecommunications firms from the low-cost Asian manufacturers, as well as from the growing size and purchasing power of competitors such as Sony Ericsson, Nortel Networks, and Siemens. In a high-stakes, highly competitive environment, this international mega-merger would be a significant test of leadership.

THE RELATIONAL CIRCUIT
Sense as a Response to Complexity

The more complex the issues that companies have to face, the more re-ductionist traditional responses tend to be. Standard recommendations to leaders include simplifying the problem, recruiting more specialized staff, or implementing linear and sequential fixes such as cost reduction and concentration on core functions. As a result, businesses often don't mea-sure up to the complexity of the challenges they face. Part of the problem lies in the question: How can we analyze something if it keeps moving?

I believe that the answer to the question of complexity is to be found outside traditional mechanisms, outside our comfort zone. We have already seen that complexity drives relationships in nonlinear ways. Organizations need to engage these same principles to stay above water, above market, and maintain a level of performance that ensures their success. Just like human beings, companies are filled with contradictions and thrive when they manage the tensions and paradoxes that give them fuel.

The savoir-relier process that helps leaders manage complexity is called the *relational circuit*. When we examine the relational circuit later in this chapter, we will see that it can be used to re-create a situation and adapt it to the future environment, adjusting details to make it more competitive and more relevant and, in the process, building sense for the organiza-tion. This mind-set and the skills and processes engaged by the relational circuit allow us to address the interactions between all components of the environment in a conscious and effective way.

The Value of Tension

On December 31, 2006, eight months after the merger, Alcatel-Lucent took the bold step of acquiring Nortel's UMTS radio access business and its related assets for $320 million cash. But the U.S. market was deteriorating and the transatlantic merger was facing internal and cultural conflicts. Facilitating relationships around the globe was not enough: doing the same thing within the company was critical. The company saw six consecutive quarters of losses and faced a terrible plunge in value, with its stock price decreasing by more than 60 percent in twenty-one months. The complexity of the Franco-American merger and dire market conditions were partly responsible for the failure. But analysts also saw the company's delay in selecting its combined technology portfolio and the loss of key people after the merger as factors of the failure.

In July 2008, both the CEO and the chairman of the board—the former CEO who had masterminded the merger—stepped down. In spite of the standard integration problems that most mergers face, some tough decisions around cost-cutting and the elimination of management and operational duplications had not been not made in due time. Moreover, the company was failing to find the sense it needed and was not capable of building a relational leadership structure that would allow the new conglomerate to thrive. More than two years after its creation, Alcatel-Lucent was still floundering.

One paradox that is common to all companies is the need for agility to adapt constantly to new challenges and the need for permanence or stability to maintain a trajectory. We all need a sense of "Where is this taking us?" A company's culture, values, image, and identity are founded on the tensions that inhabit its core. Toyota is one example of a company that has recognized the value of these tensions: "The company succeeds, we believe, because it creates contradictions and paradoxes in many aspects of organizational life. Employees have to operate in a culture where they constantly grapple with challenges and problems and must come up with fresh ideas. That's why Toyota constantly gets better. The hard and the soft innovations work in tandem. Like two wheels on a shaft that bear equal weight, together they move the company forward. Toyota's culture of contradictions plays as important a role in its success as TPS (Toyota Production System) does, but rivals and experts have so far overlooked it."[1] Sense in organizations is the cog that makes complexities and tensions work positively.

Innovation and Best Practice Are Not Enough
Ben Verwaayen, appointed CEO of Alcatel-Lucent in September 2008, was charged with building a new identity for the organization. He focused on five key targets: delivering on the benefits promised when the merger occurred; embracing "open innovation"; banishing the "us versus them" mentality that was complicating transatlantic relations and insisting that the company must act as one; making executives accountable for results; and choosing the best people for positions regardless of nationality.

He also renewed and refocused the company values upon his arrival, identifying them as accountability, "customer first," innovation, respect, and teamwork. Even if all employees recognized themselves in those values, their implementation entailed differences across local cultures, so a large internal social network called Engage was built to exchange information. It soon became an open platform for pulling together project data from different teams, sharing best practices, and engaging in dialogue across countries and divisions.

The company launched a co-creation strategy to involve its customers more closely in product development and implemented new organizational processes to facilitate internal governance. However, although Alcatel-Lucent had created flexible, agile systems, the merged entity continued to lack sense and purpose. This was particularly worrying given the ongoing economic crisis, growing competition in technology markets, and the ongoing instability felt by employees following the merger. Innovation can certainly drive progress, but it does not drive sense. Sense building is central to the question of corporate identity, which in turn is central to a company's ability to weather crises without going off the rails.

Verwaayen stuck to his five-point plan through the global economic crisis and, in February 2012, was able to announce a full-year operating profit for the first time since the merger of Alcatel and Lucent. The market reacted positively, driving up share prices by 13 percent in one day, and it seemed that Alcatel-Lucent's restructuring efforts over the past three years were finally taking effect. But Verwaayen's message to employees on that Friday morning had a more sober tone: "We are not a normal company yet, we still have a lot of work to do."[2]

Indeed, the combination of softness in the European economy and a shift in the spending patterns of U.S. operators had created a hole for all equipment vendors in the last months of 2011. For Alcatel-Lucent this was painfully evident: year-on-year revenues were down in all regions and free cash flow was negative for the year by almost €500 million despite a gain of €540 million over the previous quarter. Verwaayen cautioned, "The competition outside is fierce; Alcatel-Lucent is definitely standing on a 'burning platform' and must execute to have a future."[3] An identity was forming, but sense had yet to be found.

As we will see throughout this book, when sense is not at the heart of strategy and business is overwhelmed by the instability of the present, tensions take over and distract the organization from its core objectives. With sense, the overall direction is clear, and that creates space for the paradoxes and the contradictions to exist. Even if the winds of change blow and it becomes necessary to adjust the sails, the boat stays on course. Sustainable success relies on making the connections that create this balance in spite of, or in sync with, the fluctuations that are inherent to any business. When companies have failed to make these connections, they run aground. This is what happened with Apple in the 1990s; this is what was happening with Alcatel-Lucent.

The Relational Circuit: A Five-Step Process to Build Sense

Let's turn away from Alcatel-Lucent for a moment and examine the relational circuit in more detail. We have already explored two aspects of the savoir-relier protocol: the triangular relationship between structure, freedom, and relationality that enables organizations to embrace complexity, and the three attitudes—genuine, generous, and generative—that enable leaders to build strong relationships and make confident decisions despite the tensions inherent in business and everyday life. The third aspect, the relational circuit, leverages the dynamic of relationships as a way to build sense and implement change. It has applications in many fields of

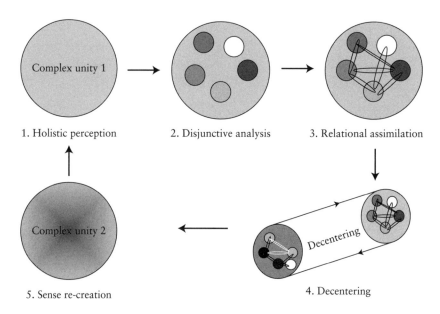

1. Holistic perception   2. Disjunctive analysis   3. Relational assimilation

Decentering

5. Sense re-creation   4. Decentering

FIGURE 4.1   Relational circuit

management, whether for solving problems, making decisions, obtaining perspective, managing change, or building sense. It can apply at different levels: at an individual level it could help a person clarify their career development goals; at an interpersonal level it could help to develop trust for conflict management; at an organizational level it could be used to create a new culture or redesign processes during a merger, acquisition, or reorganization.

The relational circuit relies on the same five-step process every time it operates at all these micro and macro levels. To see how the process works at a micro level, let's use the relational circuit to answer the question: How can you enhance your capacity to recruit effectively?

Holistic Perception: Seeing the Big Picture.   Tom is a tall, sharp-looking young man with a gentle smile on his face. You are interviewing him for a job in your unit. He walks confidently toward your desk and introduces himself in a low voice, looking you straight in the eyes. You like his style and apparent gentleness. The information gathered at this stage is intuitive and will be extremely valuable for the following steps of the relational circuit as they apply to a recruitment scenario. Looking at

Tom is like looking at an impressionist painting. You begin your relational circuit with this first impression of Tom.

Disjunctive Analysis: Zooming In to See the Parts. In order to understand your initial perception of Tom, you need to analyze the data and components that make him who he is: details of his résumé, cover letter, and references; how he answers interview questions; and so forth. The information gathered at this stage is analytical, rational, detailed, and specific. It relies on your capacity to use your cognitive, analytical, and rational skills to identify, decompose, and decode each individual piece of information that contributes to the whole.

Tom is a successful salesman who has received great reviews from former clients, but he does not have much managerial experience. He just graduated with an MBA from MIT and has a bachelor's degree in science from Oklahoma University. He was a competitive rugby player in college and has a passion for playing the piano. He formed a jazz band with friends when he was seventeen.

Relational Assimilation: Seeing How the Parts Relate to One Another. The individual components gathered in step two connect in a unique way to give you an impression of Tom as a whole individual and of how he operates. This is a sense-making exercise: you take existing components and associations and use them to discern the contradictions, conflicting ideas, or harmonies that are part of anyone's personality. It is like reading between the lines with a mix of sensibility, common sense, and rationality. Your initial intuitive perception should be challenged by the more detailed observations you have made and the data you have received. Relational assimilation draws on systems thinking and system dynamics methodologies to help understand how the complex working of these relationships gives life to the whole.[4]

In the case of Tom's recruitment, for example, you might balance his lack of management experience with his experience forming and leading a jazz band, and also give him credit for his involvement in MIT's G-Lab, where he headed a team of eight students exploring the Asian market potential for a new medication. These elements confirm your first impression that he is a person with calm energy and confidence. You have finished reading Tom; now you are ready to write a story for him in your mind.

Decentering: Writing by Projecting the Subject into the New Environment. The decentering process emerges from the three steps that you've just completed. You take into account the diverse sources of information and transpose them into the job setting. You place Tom in a new environment (job, organization, culture) and project possible matches or misfits (personality, competences, style) between the candidate and the target setting. This requires a capacity to anticipate how the complex relationships, revealed by the intuitive, analytical, and relational steps, would be written in the new context.

In the case of Tom, you would seek other possible relationships in his profile that could make him a successful leader in your marketing department with fifteen senior managers. Exploring Tom's work and the reviews he received from his G-Lab professor and his peers help you imagine him as part of your marketing team. You are anticipating how easily Tom will get along with Jennifer and Peter and the difficulties he will encounter with Oren and Francesca. You consider writing up a few amendments to your organization to facilitate his integration and compensate for his youth and lack of experience.

Sense Re-creation: Fine-Tuning to Ensure That the Subject Fits In.   The final step is the act of fine-tuning that establishes new relationships between the individual and his new environment and within the individual himself. The relationships that made the individual function effectively in his original environment will inform his new relationships and the way he fits into his new environment. You decide to trust Tom's capacity to listen to people and motivate them. You trust that his high-level scientific background will inspire respect from the senior managers who will appreciate his innovative approach and ideas.

In this last step, you have built confidence and sense from the previous stages that enable you to move away from your original understanding of the person and re-create an environment that reflects your decision to hire Tom. This process is effective only when the recruiter is capable of introspection and self-criticism: at every step, the recruiter needs to question his or her subjective perception and analysis of Tom and of the situation.

Let's now consider how the relational circuit could apply at an organizational level by returning to the example of Alcatel-Lucent.

The Relational Circuit Model at the Organizational Level

As we have seen, Alcatel-Lucent, a once-great company, was struggling with the combined challenges thrown up by an ambitious international merger; shattered, fast-paced technology markets; and the financial crisis. Its survival and future success depended on its leaders' ability to build sense for the organization, its employees, and its customers.

Hope arrived in the form of a disruptive innovation from Bell Labs, the renowned research laboratory that had been attached to Lucent prior to the merger and that had continued to function as a fairly autonomous structure. Alcatel-Lucent quickly recognized the value of this innovation and, in less than a year, had transformed it into an effective product: lightRadio. This game-changing piece of technology wowed the market when it was launched at the 2012 Barcelona Wireless World Congress. It looked like Alcatel-Lucent was back.

The Wireless Division, Alcatel-Lucent's largest product division in the networks group, had driven the development process. With its strong focus on agility, pace, and co-creation, the Wireless Division has proved to be effective in developing innovative projects in a short period of time and with few resources. Like the rest of the company, the Wireless Division was operating in a context of significant economic and organizational tension. It needed to make the postmerger changes sustainable, deliver a whole new portfolio of product solutions, win new business, and serve existing customers while convincing new customers to buy. All this had to be done while meeting the corporate goal of reducing cash burn, improving margins, and making the best use of existing talent and resources. The fact that the Wireless Division had successfully developed lightRadio in this environment showed it was capable of thriving in the face of complexity. Could Alcatel-Lucent's wider postmerger organizational and structural issues be resolved by replicating the structure, and hence the success, of the Wireless Division across the rest of its divisions and countries?

Can an innovative, agile approach successfully executed by a small group of people be replicated and become the DNA of a whole company? The challenge lies in scaling up the organizational model of a small entity to reflect the needs of a whole company while maintaining a certain level of performance. It needs to be a sense-building project rather than a sense-making project. As we have seen, attempts to replicate success that simply replicate the successful entity's processes and structures have a lackluster record of success.

The savoir-relier relational circuit does, however, provide an approach to dealing with such a complex challenge. The following steps could be applied to translate the innovative, smaller structure into a model suitable for implementation on a larger scale:

1. Holistic perception. Interviews with employees from the Wireless Division would uncover how they feel about this organization and examine their overall impression of working there.

2. Disjunctive analysis. Analyzing the different components of the organization to identify the key characteristics of its culture, structure, style, values, people, and so on would provide a firmer sense of the elements that would need to be replicated to achieve a similar outcome.

3. Relational assimilation. Identifying the relationships between these components (structure and style, values and systems, people and structure, etc.) would reveal the complexity of this task but also the richness of this innovation-based division of the company.

4. Decentering. The resulting profile of the Wireless Division could then be projected onto the whole organization. This stage is not a copy and paste but rather a mindful exercise where the relationships between the different components of the whole organization are assessed against the relationships of the Wireless Division. Gaps, similarities, and frictions would show how and where the transfer could be made possible.

5. Sense re-creation. Action could now be undertaken to build the relationships and create the new environment. The transfer of effective relationships would generate change through the development of new relationships that would translate the new culture across the organization, building sense for the business and its people. The newly formed relationships would serve as the engine of change for the organization to foster a spirit of innovation and stimulate growth.

Instead, Alcatel-Lucent is struggling to keep its head above water, lost then regained its position in the CAC 40 (the top 40 companies in the

French stock market) while hundreds of patents—patents that were valuable enough for Goldman Sachs to trust them as collateral to finance the company's debt—lie unused. The company's approach to innovation remained too passive for it to surmount the crisis. Applying the relational circuit could have unlocked the wealth of invention of which it is capable.

INNOVATION: THE WAY TO ACT WITH SENSE
Connecting the Dots

The word *innovation* has often been associated with Apple. There are many good reasons for this, even though Apple is not, of course, the only innovator in our world. The reason I am choosing Apple to illustrate how savoir-relier is a driver for innovation lies in the surprising humility the company has shown when talking about creativity and innovation. Apple's vision of innovation is embedded in Steve Jobs's simple words: "connecting the dots," another way of saying "building sense out of relationships." While it is true that Jobs used to say that there is no need to ask the consumers what they want because anticipation and surprise would foster their needs, Apple does not view innovation as a magical ability to anticipate the needs of consumers. Instead, Apple's capacity to make innovative products is the result of two key factors: a sensible vision and hard work.

The vision is above all perceptive or sensible. It comes from simple, close observation of the world and its inhabitants and the application of sensitivity and common sense to transform those observations into material concepts. For example, the vision for the iPod was "all my music in my pocket." Thereafter it is a question of hard work to make the vision come to life. This requires reliance and resilience: experimentation, trials and errors, sharing ideas, challenging proposals, making mistakes, starting over, creating hundreds of prototypes before the final product emerges. The four relationality principles of savoir-relier—perception, reliance, resilience, responsibility—are fundamental to both phases.

Innovation at Apple also goes hand in hand with influence: the company's products shape new behaviors that, in turn, generate new products and new behaviors. In this sense, innovation induces a sense of responsibility because of the organization's relationship with and influence on society.

Innovators leverage relationality to generate a product from their initial vision. The initial vision is derived from experiences, observations, and objects that do not necessarily have anything in common but in which the innovator is able to detect possible connections and relationships that give rise to an idea that can be turned into a new experience or a new product. Teasing out these connections and relationships—connecting the dots—is hard work that requires perception and resilience and, above all, requires a particular mind-set.

One example of this approach is the MagSafe system, which Apple developed to connect the power cord to its laptops. With a traditional plug-in system, if someone inadvertently snags the power cord, the laptop stays attached to the power cord and, as a result, tends to come crashing to the floor; with MagSafe, the magnetic end of the power cord detaches and the laptop stays where it is. Apple has made effective use of the magnet system but did not invent it. The company encourages its engineers to travel the world to observe and discover new ideas. One of them, on a trip to China, noticed that the rice cookers at roadside stalls used a magnet system so that the boiling water wouldn't be spilled if someone snagged the power cord. He was impressed by the usefulness of this concept and made a sense-relational move, translating the role of the magnet on the Chinese rice cookers, which protected people from being scalded, to a new and different environment and a different purpose: protecting computers from accidental damage. A combination of intuition, perception, analysis of relationships (the magnet and its function), and decentering enabled the engineer to re-create the magnet for a new environment.

Apple's "connecting things" approach is at the center of the innovation process. The power of association is critical to innovation, which depends on connecting diverse things or ideas in new ways. Varied life experiences, a sense of observation, and a sensibility to the world all enhance your capacity to innovate. New ideas emerge from the connection of different experiences. Openness, curiosity, and attentiveness, as well as empathy and generosity, are critical to building these experiences that are the source from which connections are derived.

Picasso once said: "Good artists copy, great artists steal." He did not mean that great artists had no ideas; he meant that their great ideas come from outside the world of art, from different environments, from diverse sources. Creativity is essentially a decentering process: the artist is able to decenter the relationships formed between observations of external objects and his or her internal perception and build sense in the form of new and unique ideas. Companies like Apple, with its "connecting the dots," or Google, with its "idea scouts" and "idea connectors," provide an environment for creativity and openness. They build a culture of innovation that values people who scout ideas and connect them to develop new products and make an impact on society. We will later see how the savoir-relier protocol helps develop this capacity for making unusual and improbable connections.

The Benefits of Collective Improvisation

Let's now look at how creativity and improvisation boost organizational performance. Dusya Vera and Mary Crossan show that "improvisation has a positive effect on team innovation when combined with team and contextual moderating factors."[5] The good news is that, as with savoir-relier, collective improvisational skills can be learned: "our results shed light on the opportunities provided by training in improvisation and on the challenges of creating behavioral change going beyond the individual to the team and, ultimately, to the organization."[6] In other words, spontaneity works best when the skills and techniques that underpin it have been prepared and rehearsed.

Team memory is the term used in improvisational theater to refer to a troupe's collective memory about past scenes that actors can recombine and exploit in future improvisations. Team memory has parallels with corporate procedures and systems, and its principles of free association and reincorporation provide useful lessons for business. Honda, for example, successfully improvised a strategy to introduce 50-cc bikes to the U.S. market by recombining existing marketing and sales routines.

Improvisation, like intuition, leverages experience, past sensations, and lived moments to guide action in a spontaneous way. People can make a conscious choice to allow themselves to improvise, to trust their intuition. For teams, the confidence built from experience and the trust induced by shared moments help them focus on the moment and enable them to work together and take creative action more easily and more rapidly in complex or ambiguous situations. The improvisational intention can also be present in research and development, for example, to help teams create a prototype of a new product under time pressure.

Interestingly, the work of Vera and Crossan demonstrates that the teamwork skills required for improvisation converge with the savoir-relier skills presented earlier: they include "trust among players, a common goal, a shared responsibility, a common vocabulary, and the ability both to lead and to follow."[7] Vera and Crossan argue that workplaces should be collaborative environments where both cognitive factors (shared mental models) and affective factors (trust, respect, and mutual support) contribute to highly effective, team-based innovation and performance. They advocate a culture of action where minimal structures provide the necessary freedom for experimentation to flourish. Presence (the "here and now"), vigilance, and attention are also conditions for effective collective improvisation. In fact, the only element that is missing relative to the savoir-relier approach is our focus on sensibility and sensitivity. From this practical approach where improvisational theater inspires ways to develop a culture of innovation with savoir-relier, let us return to an organizational model based on innovation: the I-form organization.

Innovation at the Structural, Organizational Level

"The I-form organizational design enables firms, especially firms that learn how to interact collaboratively within networks and communities, to compete effectively in complex and challenging environments. For a firm to be successful in such environments, it must have, or be able to develop, the capability to continually create, share, and apply knowledge."[8]

As we saw in Chapter 1, U-form organizations rely on planning and control, M-form organizations rely on delegation, and I-form organizations rely on collaboration. We are now seeing I-form companies experimenting with new designs of collaborative networks and communities driven by entrepreneurial R&D and the Internet. Technical and Computing Graphics (TCG Group), for example, is a network of innovative Australian firms that has developed a collaboration-driven business model; according to a 2009 *California Management Review* article, "TCG considered both its linkages among internal firms and its relationships with principal customers and technology partners to be learning opportunities sustained by trusting, mutually beneficial interactions. . . . Thus, partly by design and partly through ongoing trust-building, multi-firm networks evolved into 'extended enterprises' that looked more and more like collaborative federations or communities."[9]

The article cited here presents other examples of companies that are successfully engaged in collaborative communities, such as Syndicom in the health sector and Blade.org in information technology. In the case of Syndicom, surgeons have decided to create collaborative platforms to share their expertise, experience, and ideas. The "CollabComs" in operation have demonstrated that "trust-based knowledge sharing and utilization among a community of professionals and related firms can be deliberately designed and activated quickly and efficiently."[10] While such collaborative processes usually occur spontaneously and are not necessarily sustainable, the case of Syndicom and other similar collaborative communities shows that structure and design can function with free, individual, and spontaneous contributions. The question then became whether the model could be replicated in any context.

Eight companies, including IBM and Intel, founded Blade.org in 2006 to develop software solutions around IBM's new Blade technology. The approach is different from that of Syndicom since it was consciously founded by an organization rather than developing organically from individual initiatives. Interestingly, IBM plays the role of facilitator but has left leadership of the group to other members. The Blade.org example shows that "a complete market exploration business model can be efficiently and effectively pursued by organizing a collaborative community of complementary firms."[11] The 2009 *California Management Review* article concludes that both trusting relationships and collaborative skills lead to effective knowledge sharing and argues that "fast" and "caring" trust can be facilitated and sustained through a mix of experience and processes or protocols.

Tracing economic evolution and the business models that come to the fore in different periods is a good way to analyze how companies have responded over time to the needs of society and the market. The emergence

and growing success of collaborative communities as a new form of organization supports the argument that structure, freedom, and relationality
have much to offer in the current environment, which, as we have seen,
is characterized by complexity and speed. The I-form organization, with
its focus on innovation, provides clear markers for organizations seeking
to establish collaborative, generative structures that are compatible with
the savoir-relier model. The I-form does not, however, reflect the need for
organizations to build sense for their employees and for society at large. I
believe that the need for sense will become clear as we move forward and
companies take steps to integrate sustainability and responsibility into the
generative dimension. While sustainable innovation may appear to be an
oxymoron, innovation, along with sense and responsibility, is an engine
of change with the power to make economic, environmental, and social
imperatives an integral part of corporate strategy.

Sustainability Is an Imperative

Most companies today have a sustainable development or corporate social
responsibility statement on their website. In many cases these statements are
simply a fashionable way to "fit in" and pay lip service to public opinion
or government measures. Sustainability and responsibility should, however, be a key component of the company as a living dynamic ecosystem
and, as such, an integral part of its corporate governance and strategy. A
company that has a genuine identity and vision for its future necessarily
has an eye on sustainability and projects its activities over the long term.

Companies address sustainable development in different ways depending on their strategy, their priorities, and their values. They also have to
take account of the diverse, and often conflicting, needs and expectations
of their stakeholders. Again, we find the need to embrace complexity and
find sense. Companies have to make difficult trade-offs in order to reconcile the economic, social, and environmental impacts of their decisions.
This "triple bottom line" is challenging because it means looking at the
world of business in a different way, with an awareness of the whole and
of our responsibility toward society.

Companies must manage the complexity of multiple interactions
while maintaining a defined trajectory and balancing the often conflicting

requirements of the three imperatives of the triple bottom line. Let us look at the example of Shell, the Anglo-Dutch petrochemical company, to understand how savoir-relier can be used to integrate sustainability and responsibility into corporate strategy.

The Example of Shell.   Shell faced two major challenges in the 1990s that generated huge amounts of negative publicity and had a significant impact on the group's strategy. The first was the decision to sink the Brent Spar, a redundant oil storage installation in the North Sea. This was met with a storm of public protest, led by Greenpeace; in the end, Shell was forced to reverse its decision and dismantle the platform on the mainland, even though it argued that the initial plan to sink the platform was the more environmentally friendly of the two options.

Then, a few years later, the company hit the headlines again with a serious crisis in Nigeria, where it ran significant operations and had made important investments. In 1995, Ken Saro-Wiwa, a human rights activist and leader of the Movement for the Survival of the Ogoni People (MOSOP), and eight other Ogoni leaders were executed by the Nigerian government following a nonviolent campaign against the oil-related environmental degradation of Ogoniland and what they perceived as the government's failure to enforce environmental regulations against foreign companies extracting the oil, notably Shell. Their execution was widely condemned and generated huge emotion around the world. Shell was accused of not intervening to influence the decision of the military government and was criticized for carrying on its operations in Nigeria despite the situation.

The public outcry came as a shock to Shell, which prided itself on being a principled company and had operated according to its "Business Principles" for more than twenty years. How could a company that claimed strong ethical values fall so short of public expectations? Shell needed to find the resilience to draw lessons from what happened. The company launched a major initiative, determined to do whatever it took to ensure that a similar situation never arose again.

Shell embarked on a major engagement exercise with its stakeholders, who included nongovernmental organizations (NGOs), academics, suppliers, and governments. The board decided to integrate sustainable development into every dimension of the business, and a sustainable development group was created to ensure that the strategy the board had identified would be properly implemented across the organization and embedded in the very culture of the company. This group embodied the company's quest to build sense: "we have a continuing program of aligning key business processes with a governance framework of commitments, policies, standards and guidelines consistent with contributing to sustainable development. We call this 'hardwiring.'"[12]

The interesting aspect of Shell's approach is its desire to balance hardwiring with "softwiring": "we are building the capacity of Shell people through communications, leadership development programs and competency frameworks designed to encourage sustainable development thinking and behavior. To achieve real change, it is important to reach the hearts and minds of the people. Informal networks can play a significant complementary role."[13] The association of "hard" and "soft" approaches reflects the need to balance rational and emotional approaches in management and strategy. The process Shell engaged in addressed those two dimensions in parallel. However, the sensible dimension is not addressed in Shell's model. Neither totally rational nor emotional, the sensible dimension would enhance the level and quality of awareness that Shell people could achieve.

Even so, Shell developed a process of sense making, referring explicitly to Karl Weick's theory, to clarify what sustainable development meant to its business. This would ensure that every employee in the company understood and bought into the journey. The process of sense making was built around four stages to translate sustainability as a concept into action items that fit with the company's language and underpinned a common sense of purpose.[14] Those stages have significant parallels with the principles of relationality and the relational circuit:

1. Sensitizing (perception): building awareness of and sensibility to issues relating to corporate responsibility.

2. Discovering (building from resilience with agility): capturing a real sense of the value and engagement associated with sustainability and responsibility by experimenting with small initiatives and projects.

3. Embedding, that is, hardwiring (reliance): linking in with structural and systemic aspects of the business.

4. Routinizing, that is, softwiring (reliance and responsibility): linking corporate responsibility to the company's core business.

The power of Shell's approach lies in its capacity to take the social, environmental, and financial dimensions of sustainable development and weave them into the varied systems, structures, and processes of the group. This was done through a sustained process of engagement—communication, training, and skill development—that gradually gave sense to the whole sustainability/responsibility journey. A number of knowledgeable and enthusiastic change agents acted as connectors, developing formal and informal internal networks to share the new approach at all levels of the organization. In this sense, both "savoir" and "relier" were at the core of Shell's approach to embed sustainability and responsibility among the workforce and within its structures and procedures.

Genuine Efforts Result in Cultural Change.   Almost twenty years after these incidents, Shell continues to prioritize sustainable development in its management model. The structural changes that the company implemented, including a dedicated social responsibility committee to oversee issues at board level, have allowed it to question and review its business policies in light of global issues such as climate change. Shell has also created biodiversity standards with decision-making impacts and set up a Social Performance Management Unit, which aims "to develop meaning around our social impacts and create tools and techniques to minimize negative impacts, create long-lasting economic benefits, and contribute more generally to the wellbeing of communities and broader society."[15]

The genuine efforts made by Shell to integrate and model its strategy with a sustainability/responsibility lens have had a positive impact on its performance. At the Norco chemical plant in New Orleans and the Nanhai Petrochemicals development in China, for instance, financial investments to upgrade the sites have positively impacted the environment and the local economy, while open and direct communication and principled engagement with all stakeholders, including local people and communities and state and government officials, have created business value.

Finally, the introspection that underpinned Shell's philosophy and actions has fostered a model that relies on theories and principles and is open to inspire others. As a result, by innovating with a new business model, Shell is also influencing business as a whole, beyond its industry. Companies that manage to bind sustainability and responsibility with sense have a positive influence on society. Adding perception and sensibility to enhance awareness would further increase the positive impact of their strategy.

The Reality of Savoir-Relier Organizations

In terms of individual leadership, evolution has been fairly limited. In 2008, three professors from Berkeley and INSEAD launched a global project to develop a scorecard that would select the best-performing CEOs in the world. In the conclusion to the latest iteration of the scorecard,[16] the researchers contend that short-term emphasis will remain the rule of business so long as methods for evaluating performance remain focused on profits and return on investments. This is particularly true in times of crises, when the short-term interests of both the company and its leaders tend to take precedence over long-term concerns for obvious reasons of survival. Unless performance measures of long-term and non-financial results are integrated into scorecards and compensations or benefits, the world will keep on considering moneymakers the gods or heroes of business. Thankfully, the study makes a step toward more long-term, global, and "doing well/doing good" considerations, paving the way for the possibility of new and postheroic analyses.

Building sense is a continuous effort, a search for something that is to be found within yourself again and again. Your sense of purpose is the combination of personal introspection confronted by external reality, in the form of people and events. By looking around and opening yourself up to different ways of thinking and acting, you can forge your own approach and your own sense. It is by confronting reality that you can build a more solid and reliable understanding of your own sense and how it operates. The same goes with sense in organizations, only on a larger scale. Unfortunately, like people, many companies just don't know how to maintain a consistent sense in the face of necessary change.

THE SAVOIR-RELIER

ORGANIZATION

Generating Performance and Sustainable Growth

An interesting example of sense building lies with the *Mittelstand* (small and medium enterprises [SMEs] or family businesses) that are said to be the real economic force behind Germany's growth. To quote the CEO of a *Mittelstand* company, speaking in June 2012: "The reason why our company exists is because my purpose is to deliver a company to my children and relatives, one that will be thriving in even better ways than it was when I took over. This is why our family business is so strong in such sustainable way. . . . We make sure the next generations will be excited to carry on the mission we have started."[1]

This leader builds sense in the act of preparing for the time when he will hand over a successful company to his heirs; he implied that he considered the company's employees to be as much part of that family as his actual relatives. His comments prompted a question from the audience: "What if there is no one from the family who wants to carry on?" His answer: "We make sure as our children grow up that at least one will be good for the company. We find other paths for the ones who are not seen as good for the company."[2] The CEO acknowledged, "It has been difficult recently because there have been fewer births in the family but we have a strong sense of solidarity and this approach has worked for over six generations so far."[3] The implied attachment and sensibility to what the company represents at a symbolic level as well as its ability to provide a concrete source of revenue for the family accounts for the sense that lies behind his desire to build and grow the company.

TOWARD A NEW FORM OF ORGANIZATION

What is the optimal structure to foster the savoir-relier organization? And how does savoir-relier drive organizational performance? In addressing these questions, we are moving from the individual dimension of savoir-relier to its organizational and social dimensions. An organization needs structure on which to build an identity to generate performance and sustainable growth; it anchors its identity and values in the people it recruits and develops in a spirit of collaboration, trust, and confidence. The capacity of savoir-relier organizations to absorb and work with the tensions of globalization, change, and complexity is characteristic of the relational force that drives its people.

The three attributes identified to characterize the savoir-relier leader—genuine, generous, and generative—can also apply to the savoir-relier organization. The genuine dimension underpins the need for the organization to develop self-awareness and confidence through its history and to create open and fluid channels of communication. The generous dimension embeds diversity in the structure of the organization and encourages collaboration and trust through networks. Finally, the generative dimension fosters innovation that builds sense and moves value from organization to society, introducing sustainable development and responsibility as an integral component of organizational strategy.

With the generative side of the organization, we dive into the link between relationality and sense. The genuine and generous sides assert the confidence, the identity, and the trust-based collaborative dimension. However, these attributes are not sufficient to build the savoir-relier organization; sense is what makes a difference. Sense is what drives organizations to the next stage, moving from innovation to influence. Sense is what brings everything together.

The Difference between a Company and an Institution

Rosabeth Moss Kanter speaks of "institutional logic" to highlight how great companies anchor their business in society, politics, economics, religion, and community to build enduring institutions.[4] The very notion of an "institution" is what distinguishes companies that build their success on short-term profit from those that build a durable and coherent identity. Institutions base their leadership on relationships that are built around sense; that sense is found not only within the business but also beyond it. Institutions consider themselves an active part of a living ecosystem within which they share responsibility for economic, social, and environmental performance.

Kanter argues that six markers distinguish institutions from companies: a common purpose, a long-term view, emotional engagement, community building, innovation, and self-organization. PepsiCo, Procter & Gamble, Novartis, and IBM are all companies that can be considered institutions. For example, in line with its stated aim of "improving more lives in more places more completely," Procter & Gamble's Baby Care Group has set up Pampers mobile clinics in West Africa to reduce infant mortality. Novartis employees spend time in hospitals to see and understand better how their drugs are used so they can adapt and innovate with a better sense of the actual needs. In times of crisis—for example, after the Asian tsunami, Hurricanes Katrina and Sandy in the United States, and earthquakes in China and Japan—IBM provided software support to track relief supplies.

Kanter's observations converge to some extent with the savoir-relier approach by showing that organizations and their leaders can generate sustainable growth while upholding their responsibility toward society. The companies cited are clearly moving in the right direction, but do these examples show a complete mind-set shift toward sense? Are those companies genuinely involved in a generous move to generate performance with sense?

If we return to the examples of our three leaders and look at how they manage their organization, we find echoes of the six markers identified by Kanter. Clara Gaymard was an ambassador for GE International and traveled the world as the GE City Initiative Leader to meet with national officials and advise on sustainable urban development. Pascal Cagni's mission at Apple EMEIA impacted both the business and society, helping to make the iPhone into an icon in most European countries, facilitating access to education and information in Eastern European and African countries, and contributing to the development of innovative educational platforms like iTunes U and K12 as well as to the Apple Premium Resellers business model. Apollonia Poilâne runs an organization with long-established values and a tradition of quality while innovating to increase the happiness and well-being of her customers through the simple medium of bread. We will return to these three examples of savoir-relier leadership later to assess how they have handled organizational change. But let us first better understand how the three characteristics of the savoir-relier leader apply to organizations.

Developing a Savoir-Relier Mind-Set: Working with Tensions
We have seen how the inherent tension between structure and freedom can drive successful innovation and creativity in business, how a savoir-relier mind-set leverages those tensions by stimulating a desire to share and express the individual differences that form the wealth of the organization, and that while organizations need to build structures and processes that leave room for individual expression, they also need to bind those same individuals to a sense of collective identity with shared goals and common rules. Within organizations as with the individual, the triangular association between structure, freedom, and relationality serves as the engine for the organization to adopt a savoir-relier mind-set and is founded on the four relationality principles of perception, reliance, resilience, and responsibility.

Structure, freedom, and relationality are the keys to successful savoir-relier leadership. Structure is key because the organization needs a sound framework and strong values in the form of processes, strategy, vision, and so forth. Freedom is key because autonomy and initiative foster action in the form of innovation and creativity. And relationality is key because it anchors the organization to its foundation and facilitates the dynamic and systemic movement of the organization in the living ecosystem. Relationality triggers change.

THE GENUINE ORGANIZATION IMBUED WITH SELF-AWARENESS AND CONFIDENCE
Bridging Divides and Sharing Values
At the macro level of an organization, the ecosystem is relatively fragile because nature tends to group people around sets of actions and values that build cohesion and separate them from other groups, even if they live

under the same "roof." In society, the human need for belonging is expressed through the formation of families, tribes, and nations; the separation that confirms that sense of belonging can lead to everything from gang fights to civil wars. In organizations, our need for belonging can easily result in silos, which lead to internal competition and isolation, both of which challenge the balance of the ecosystem. Isolated parts of the company tend to generate isolated groups, then isolated individuals who think they do better, know better, or act better. The sense of collective identity and the sense of purpose are lost and the focus shifts to individual interest.

Savoir-relier helps generate a mind-set of collaboration and relational coordination that weaves across divisions in time and space to prevent silos from developing or break them down where they exist already.

Pernod Ricard, for example, has launched a university where leadership development programs include savoir-relier seminars to grow the mind-set of sharing, individual and collective attention, care, and respect for others in line with their "conviviality" value set. Once the ecosystem operates around a solid set of collaborative and relational principles that are embedded in individual and collective actions, the organization's leadership must make sure that those relationality principles are sustainable, that is, able to survive and adapt in time and space, across boundaries, and in the face of challenges.

The i-Share portal at Pernod Ricard is intended to inform and grow the group's leadership values and foster a mind-set of conviviality. It is but one example of the kind of concrete action that can be taken to decentralize business units around shared values, such as entrepreneurship, innovation, and ethical collaboration, while maintaining a central core identity.[5] Companies that have understood that their most important assets are their people are in a better position to work on the relational dynamics that will make the ecosystem perform. Strong relationships built on trust and respect at the individual, group, organizational, and societal levels are the foundation of performance and results.

History as an Identity Builder

The importance of self-awareness at the organizational level is linked to the need to build a corporate identity that fosters a sense of belonging to the corporate community and grows confidence in the company values among employees. The motivation and engagement of employees is often tied to the feeling that "This is where I belong," "I am in the right place," or "I sense a fit with the way people behave and think."

Knowing and understanding the history of the company anchors this sense of belonging in the values that drive a common purpose and orient the company's future goals. History shapes the culture of the company. History brings sense to corporate decisions by joining the original *raison d'être* of the company, often attached to its name and to the genuine values that motivated its creation and drove its development, with the movements of time and change that all lasting companies must incorporate in their sustainable growth. Family businesses that grow with mergers and acquisitions, that welcome new shareholders and new board and executive committee members, yet still carry their original name and manage to maintain an identity over time are a case in point.

Pernod Ricard has a strong history to build from strong, established values of entrepreneurship and conviviality. Paul Ricard, the company's founder, invented the anise-flavored liqueur that bears his name, and his son, Patrick, further developed the company. In 1975, Ricard merged with its competitor Pernod. This act of relationality was a smart move that made the company strong enough to start its worldwide expansion, a path that has been followed with the same entrepreneurial spirit that characterized the company's origins and the motto, "local roots, global reach." The company's values of sharing, conviviality, and innovation have been extended to all of the companies acquired by the group over the years.

Two books relate the history of the company and an annual event is held in Les Embiez, the island owned by the Ricard family, at which more than eight hundred people gather to celebrate the company's tradition and spirit as well as its results and objectives. Conviviality, or "the art of living together," is inscribed in the corporate signature, *créateurs de convivialité*, and gives a genuine, human dimension to the company.

History as a Driver of Purpose
Communication channels such as books, websites, and events are opportunities for people to remember where a company comes from and give

them an opportunity to unite around values they understand and can relate to. History here is the relational glue that binds people together in the
corporate community. This relationality fosters initiatives and innovation
because the security it provides is a source of confidence for members of
the organization. Pernod Ricard's solid foundation is associated with a
strong entrepreneurial spirit thanks to the group's history of motivating
and engaging its members in developing new products and inventing new
approaches to their business. The integration process for new recruits in-
corporates processes to help them absorb and identify with the corporate
culture and values. History, through its relationality function, can facilitate
change by creating a sense of community and belonging.

As the American historian and philosopher Carl Becker wrote, "The
past is a kind of screen upon which each generation projects its vision of
the future."[6] In an article in the *Harvard Business Review* in 2012, John T.
Seaman Jr. and George David Smith, two scholars who hold PhDs in history, argued that "communicating the history of the enterprise can instill
a sense of identity and purpose and suggest the goals that will resonate."[7]
They suggest the following practices to "put history on your side": visiting
corporate archives, interviewing departing executives, surveying what is
known and understood about the company's values and history, making
the history accessible, learning from both failures and successes, seeking
historical perspective before every major decision, and talking about history at every opportunity. They added, "history offers pragmatic insights,
valid generalizations and meaningful perspectives."[8]

Seaman and Smith gave many examples of how companies have successfully used history to foster strategic action and decisions. They mentioned
Kraft and Cadbury aligning their parallel histories to facilitate their merger,
UPS referring to the many previous transformations they had undergone to
ease acceptance for significant new changes in the 1990s, and IBM CEO
Samuel Palmisano, who was a history major in college, coining core values from IBM's history while getting rid of the emotional attachment to
past successes. At IBM the result was a corporate history that highlighted
the company's ability to make breakthrough innovations and combined it
with the original values of "satisfying customer needs and building long-
term relationships."[9] These ideas became drivers for change that resulted

in consensus over the Smarter Planet Initiative and numerous innovations in technology and collaborative design.

Communication: the Voice and Soul of an Organization
Communication plays a major role in the process of establishing how a company's values and structures relate to its history. At the individual level, transparency, authenticity, and straight talk were identified as signs of genuineness that facilitate effective communication and dialogue in savoir-relier leadership. Clear and fluid communication also characterizes a genuine and healthy company. A company that is not confident in its vision and direction does not tend to communicate effectively. Communication is not a marketing tool, at least not in the savoir-relier model. The way a company expresses itself and the words and images it chooses to represent itself are a reflection of its identity, its personality. The genuine organization has a voice that is the expression of its soul.

In practice, this voice manifests itself in a variety of ways, through obvious channels such as official press releases and statements but also indirectly, through the values that are embodied by the members of the organization. What is said about a company is one thing, how it is said another, but to whom it is said is just as important. Communication being a two-way street, audience is a critical component to consider when delivering messages and sharing ideas. The CEO of an organization may communicate certain things in one way to the press and in another to the staff, to unions, or to the board. Does this mean this CEO is a liar or a manipulator? Of course not. As we saw in our discussion of the risks of being too genuine, leaders must craft their communication with care and hold back when their words might negatively affect a situation or person or when the timing is not right. Impact and influence come with understanding what is most relevant at a given time for certain people. Just as Samuel Palmisano selected the elements in the history of IBM that were most relevant to the changes he was seeking to implement in order that the company could thrive again, a talented savoir-relier leader will select and associate the words that correspond to the genuine and relevant information that is required at a particular time. The information and image a genuine leader projects will always, however, be true to the values of his or her organization.

The Importance of Sincerity

In the savoir-relier organization, communication is characterized by sincerity, the willingness to speak the truth. Speaking with your own voice, the voice of the organization, is a sign of confidence in the values that have brought people together around a common sense of purpose and goals. This does not mean that communication needs to be spontaneous and improvised. Well-orchestrated communication is representative of the care and attention paid to the company's values and how they are translated to different audiences.

Steve Jobs's keynote addresses for Apple were renowned as perfect examples of carefully orchestrated moments of communication that reflected a genuine attachment to and representation of Apple's identity and values. Other companies like Facebook have adopted similar communication approaches. It is important to note, however, that Steve Jobs was himself in those moments: he certainly practiced and rehearsed like a performing artist but he was doing what he believed in and he presented his products in his own unique way. Pascal Cagni, CEO of Apple EMEIA, did the same when he was speaking to his audience to promote the same innovations and new products: he respected the form and structure of Steve Jobs's presentations while being himself and injecting his own personality and presence. It will be interesting to track the evolution in Apple's communications following Jobs's death. Thus far, the setting has remained the same, with keynote addresses broadcast worldwide for the launch of new products, but the voice has changed. Will that lead to a change in Apple's values? Possibly; time will tell.

Not every company relies so strongly on its CEO to embody its image. Communication is everywhere, inside and outside. Relationality is again the key to achieving the subtle balance between structure and freedom, maintaining control over the message while giving people the liberty to express themselves. People who feel good in an organization will feel confident to speak about what goes well and what does not go well inside the company. Christine Lagarde, the managing director of the International Monetary Fund (IMF), was the chairwoman of the American law firm Baker & McKenzie prior to becoming the French minister of foreign affairs. Speaking about leadership to HEC MBA students in 2005, she was asked about the role of communication in leadership and explained that at Baker & McKenzie, "members of the firm could criticize openly and freely and were even encouraged to talk about what was not well. But only inside the firm. If anyone consistently badmouthed the firm outside, no matter how long they had been with the firm, they were out. If you cannot speak positively of the company where you spend a large portion of your time and energy, then you should not be there in the first place."[10]

Channels for self-expression and sharing inside the organization abound in many forms, from informal discussions around the water cooler to formal forums, intranets, and platforms designed specifically to facilitate the exchange of ideas, opinions, and views. These channels are a means for companies to develop an internal voice, a language that is its own. These voices are different from the institutional and external voices that communicate through press releases, the corporate website, advertisements, and branding tools such as the corporate logo. Social and professional networks also spread information and communication in a less controlled, more diffuse way. Understanding and managing those tools and channels is particularly important given their potential to escape control and go viral.

Developing a savoir-relier mind-set through genuine communication is a way to work consistently across those multiple channels. Genuineness is an attitude that can drive your choices and decisions about how you communicate, regardless of the channel: what matters is that you remain true to yourself and true to your organization. Sincerity comes with the confidence that is built out of experience, successes and failures, discernment and resilience, and the capacity to have a sense of perspective in moving forward. The savoir-relier organization is genuine and connects with the audience and its true identity. The uniqueness of its values is incarnated by its employees and leaders.

Theodore Zeldin, the British historian and philosopher who wrote *Conversation*,[11] an essay that charts the power of dialogue and the need for quality exchange between human beings, once told me as we were discussing my leadership: "You mustn't compete, you must be unique." His words stayed with me throughout my time as the head of the HEC MBA and I strove to make the program unique in its content, the people it recruited, the values it relied on, and the way it communicated them. Communication is often a point of contention, an area where organizational and strategic tensions crystallize and become visible. The genuine attitude of a savoir-relier organization is transmitted directly through its communication. Thus, the company must carefully choose the words used to express its ideas, ensuring that they reflect its specific and unique identity.

Unfortunately, the corporate communications of large organizations in different sectors often use exactly the same messages and wording as each other: companies promoting their supposed uniqueness, integrity, entrepreneurship, and social responsibility do so using words that are so generic that they have lost all meaning. Effective communication requires close attention to language and a commitment to work with words that are well defined and associated in ways that are specific to that one company. They cannot be interchangeable. You should recognize a company in the way it crafts its discourse in the same way that you would recognize a painter or a poet by his or her distinctive style. This attention to detail is central to what I refer to as genuine communication.

THE GENEROUS ORGANIZATION FOUNDED ON COLLABORATION AND TRUST
Valuing Diversity in a Collaborative Environment

Diversity—in the form of charters, indicators, scorecards, affirmative action policies, antidiscrimination policies, equal-opportunity programs, and so on—is on the agenda of any company today that describes itself as socially responsible. Most of these "diversity strategies" address only the most visible, polemic, and socially important dimensions of diversity. I would argue that the reasons these initiatives do not always have the expected impact is that they have a limited concept of what diversity means. Diversity is not just about race or gender. Diversity is not just about people. Diversity is also about ideas, concepts, experiences, and senses. It is the expression of life; embracing diversity means embracing all the different facets of life. Embracing gender diversity without embracing diversity of perspectives and ideas makes no sense. The real challenge of diversity lies in the capacity of an organization not only to accept differences between people, cultures, ideas, and perspectives as a source of creativity and innovation, but to seek out and value those differences.

Diversity is becoming one of the most difficult management challenges for companies today. If companies recognize diversity as a social imperative as well as a key driver for innovation, it remains a source of complexity, conflict, and tensions that are difficult and time-consuming to manage. Success depends on building relationships between elements, people, and ideas that are apparently disconnected, conflicting, or opposite. Once again, we find the need for a savoir-relier mind-set to build sense and relationships.

The UK-based global company Reckitt Benckiser, which produces home, personal-care, and health products, claims that the diversity of its workforce is one of its strongest competitive advantages. Since 1999, when it was formed from the merger of Reckitt & Colman and Benckiser, the company has made a strong commitment to diversity. Bart Bech, the former CEO, believed in cultural diversity but also encouraged the mixing of people from different functions and generations and encouraged his managers to build project teams by selecting people who had never worked together before. The purpose was to challenge our natural inclination to work with people we know or who come from a similar background and to stimulate new ideas from new and different—sometimes diverging and conflicting—perspectives. The mix of origins and the forced composition of project teams would foster openness and tolerance for differences leading to greater effectiveness, as we saw in the case of the HEC MBA.

Bech made diversity an engine for innovation. Indeed, diversity at Reckitt Benckiser has become a dynamic dimension in the management of the workforce. Connecting people to make them work together, when they were not necessarily expecting to, has created a climate of collaboration and exploration. Diversity is understood as the opposite of routine: employees are exposed to different environments, people, and colleagues, which keeps them alert and open to change. This facilitates the emergence of innovation as well as a corporate culture of collaboration that has spread through the entire organization because it is based on genuine acts rather than on words alone.

Of course, Reckitt Benckiser is just one example of an organization that has made respect for diversity into a growth driver. Yet it remains an example to follow for other companies that wish to thrive by adopting a savoir-relier mind-set. Savoir-relier embraces diversity and welcomes differences of all sorts to generate a spirit of tolerance and openness and, ultimately, grow a culture of innovation.

The Role of Brokerage in Building Sense and Relationships

Brokerage is an interesting element to consider in questions of collective performance. It builds strong networks by connecting previously separate and sometimes conflicting parties to facilitate collaboration and coordination. Such relational practices have proven effective in organizations like the design firm IDEO, which has found success by developing a process of information access, storage, and retrieval that facilitates effective transfers of ideas from one industry to another. Brokerage is also the concept behind Google's idea connectors, which we discussed previously, and could be seen as a seventh marker of Kanter's "institutional logic" for its potential to significantly improve performance.

Brokerage in the savoir-relier sense involves more than just making connections. It means identifying ideas, synthesizing them, and anticipating where and how they could be integrated into a structure so the process of innovation can flow. As a process, brokerage can be compared to the relational circuit. The first step requires an intuitive understanding of the idea's value, which is then analyzed and broken down into its various components so the relationships between them become clear. The second step involves decentering the idea relative to the company's system so that its integration and re-creation as a new product or system can be imagined.

An ethnographic study of independent country music producers by Elizabeth Long Lingo and Siobhán O'Mahony shows brokerage in a new light by opposing the dynamic practice of brokerage to its traditionally structural position.[12] This exposes a new organizational process that bridges relational coordination in a creative environment: "creative brokerage and the process of integrating multiple, often-competing perspectives into a creative whole are common to entrepreneurial ventures, the evolution of social movements and institutions, and projects arising in creative industries such as film, theater and music."[13] The move from structure to practice highlights how information can be put to creative use. Brokers synthesize and integrate ideas to help the participants in creative projects manage ambiguity. The focus on practice implies an emphasis on actions that reflect people's understanding of how to get things done in complex settings.[14]

Brokers, however, cannot operate on their own. They need to be part of a network where people cooperate to contribute to the emergence of a public or shared good.[15] At the same time, brokers are responsible for the completion of projects. Thus, they face the tension between "the pressures for collective learning, predictability, and control, and the pressures for creative responses to new problems and opportunities."[16] Similar issues arise in organizations dealing with creative or cultural projects.

The tensions on which organizations build their power and performance are exaggerated in the context of artistic and cultural environments, because cultural goods face competing market and aesthetic perspectives that can challenge their authenticity and because cultural projects often face multiple interpretations as to what is "good."[17] As a result, they need to engage with "systems to support and market cultural products while preventing those systems from suppressing individual inspiration and creativity."[18]

Lingo and O'Mahony argue for a process model of collective creativity. They found that the management of ambiguity is the engine of what they call "nexus work," which occurs over four phases, each of which gives rise to different forms of ambiguity. These phases are resource gathering, definition of project boundaries, creative production, and final synthesis.[19] In the resource-gathering phase, the ambiguity relates to the quality of the artist and his or her songs. Producers have to build the perception of potential success by fostering a generative network that builds legitimacy for the project and reduces doubts—ambiguity—about quality. Their key challenge here is to assemble a set of songs and build the perception that the artist will be commercially successful; the quality of the song portfolio will determine the move to the next phase.

In the second phase, ambiguity over claims of expertise and control becomes more acute as all contributors maintain competing perceptions as to which songs have "hit" potential. The producers' key challenge is then to select the songs that will be recorded without disenfranchising contributors to the project. In the creative production phase, more experts become involved and a new ambiguity emerges around how to transform individual contributions into a coherent whole. In the final synthesis phase, the producers move out of the studio to work with the engineer and bring the project to completion. Only a broad set of nexus practices adapting to the type of ambiguity faced at a given time would reduce ambiguity. When a transformation process is involved, the focus is on building creative capacity rather than trying to reduce ambiguity in order to preserve relationships and the conditions to foster experimentation, risk-taking, and creative work.

This example of brokerage in creative contexts highlights the importance of adaptive capacity in network relationships. But ambiguity is present in any organization. Savoir-relier organizations must deal with the ambiguity that arises when combining the positional power that leadership entails with an environment that motivates individual contributions in order to create a cohesive and coherent whole.

To return to the example, country music industry producers must use their positional power to connect to others and build trust while facilitating creativity, but also separate and control when and how people are involved in the creative process in order to effectively represent all interests and achieve collective creative performance. The relationship between the role of the producer as both leader and broker highlights the importance of linking individual roles to organizational structures so as to serve or benefit the collective. The case of producers resembles that of our savoir-relier leaders who alternate between different roles and move from a structural leadership position to a role of mediator or translator, who integrates and synthesizes before producing.

The case of country music producers may appear narrow. Indeed it is embedded in dense, small networks that probably accentuate the need to engage in relational practices to drive creative innovation in a cultural context. However, the degree of complexity involved reflects similar settings in possibly larger networks. Brokerage appears to be an effective means to connect and apply relational coordination practices in other complex and high-risk environments.

Relational coordination research and practice presents alternative models to the collaborative communities presented earlier, namely

Syndicom in the health sector and Blade.org in information technology. Recent research shows that "relational coordination, co-production and leadership involve facilitative, supportive, and connective behaviors between workers, customers and managers. By embedding caring and relational competences within performance frameworks, formal structures can support these practices as legitimate."[20]

The proposed frameworks include identification and training for relational competence, cross-role performance measures and rewards, structured cross-role conflict resolution, relational job design, cross-role meetings or relational space, and flexible cross-role protocols to embed reciprocal interrelating into worker, customer, and manager roles. The context of studies involves organizations with high reliability needs, such as those in the health care sector or airline industry.

THE GENERATIVE ORGANIZATION DRIVING INNOVATION AND INFLUENCE

Let's return to our three savoir-relier leaders and see how they have managed to help grow their organizations. Each of them is operating in their own complex environment, but all of them share the same desire to build sense.

General Electric as a Generative Organization

As an organization, General Electric demonstrates many genuine, generous, and generative features. It has evolved over time thanks to people who have committed their energy and talent to driving the business forward and improving our environment.

Clara Gaymard's leadership at General Electric has led to significant growth for the company's French business and supported GE's shift toward a strategy driven by green and responsible business. Large investments in health care research, for example, have made France the largest global supplier of new mammogram equipment. In energy, another significant innovation carried out in France is a new gas power plant, Flexefficiency 50, which is the first natural gas–fueled plant to achieve 61 percent energy efficiency at a time when the best coal-fired plants achieve only 45 percent. GE's investments in health, transport, and energy share a common objective: to improve people's lives. The "ecomagination" and "healthymagination" concepts were designed at the organizational level to characterize this commitment, whether by reducing CO_2 emissions and carbon footprint, developing the energy-efficient locomotive or airplane engines of tomorrow, or creating the medical diagnosis tools that will help save thousands of people's lives.

As GE's International City Initiative Leader, Clara Gaymard was closely involved in larger corporate initiatives to understand the needs of emerging cities and help respond to their rapid growth with solutions that help them move faster, in a direction that is also beneficial to the world at large. Shanghai is one of the fastest growing cities on our planet, but also one of the most polluting. As International City Initiative Leader, Gaymard was tasked with observing and listening to the communities and governments of cities like Shanghai to help GE understand the future needs of these urban environments, which will soon account for 80 percent of the world's production and 75 percent of its population. GE aims to contribute to their growth by proposing infrastructures that reduces the environmental impact of these megacities while also providing healthier and safer communities for their inhabitants.

These objectives are not incompatible with doing profitable business. As Gaymard argues when she is challenged by journalists about the difficult economic situation in Europe, "we must share the wealth, but let's create wealth before we share it." Innovation or invention has been one of the key drivers in the history of GE since Edison. True to its history and conscious of its identity, GE's recent "global innovation barometer" is exploring how the perception of innovation is changing in a complex globalized environment, offering a platform for companies that are looking to innovate across boundaries.

Jeffrey Immelt, CEO of GE since 2001, is constantly thinking about innovation and has been working to shift the lines of GE's business model from processes toward a more agile and fluid structure. Formerly a more process-oriented company, GE is now developing a new approach to objective-setting that is based on the real needs of employees at any given time. The introduction of greater freedom is very much in line with the idea of "making people grow" by giving them more autonomy, which is one of Gaymard's management mottos. Her role as a translator and mediator between the culture and language of a large American company and other nations, particularly France, shows the power of a genuine, generous, and generative mind-set.

Savoir-relier is a key component in GE's success. Taking it to the next level will require a conscious effort to spread this savoir-relier mind-set to GE's 300,000 employees around the world. As we will see later, the savoir-relier protocol offers simple ways to achieve this goal. For now, let us now turn to another example of savoir-relier organization with Apple.

Apple EMEIA: A Savoir-Relier Story?

Working within a giant company with a mythic name like Apple requires a respect for certain conditions. The company is highly centralized with a very strong identity and detailed, specific rules about everything from communication to product launches. In this context, regions, divisions, and units must adapt constantly to decisions and strategy handed down from the headquarters. They have little room for their own management initiatives.

Pascal Cagni, however, never tired of proposing new ways of doing business. He was daring, creative, and extremely energetic and pushed his ideas and initiatives, sometimes in challenging ways, despite the relatively rigid corporate structure within which he found himself. Between 2001 and 2012, under his leadership, the five thousand employees of Apple EMEIA achieved the most profitable growth of the whole company, with turnover from the fifty countries in the region rising from $1.3 billion to $40 billion.

As well as defending his own ideas, "the Frenchy" made a point of playing an active role in the company's strategic development team rather than acting simply as a vice president for sales. For example, he convinced Steve Jobs to launch the Apple Premium Resellers (APR), a network of 1,800 nonfranchised resellers who are now dedicated to the Apple ecosystem and create $8 billion in turnover. In Europe, Apple started collaborating with major media groups to develop a new strategy for selling iTunes content, applying its processes to emerging markets, and adding India to the EMEA portfolio in 2008. Apple EMEIA was constantly challenging the corporate headquarters, moving the lines, and convincing the centralized corporate structure to decentralize and try new avenues.

Does this make Apple EMAIA a "savoir-relier organization"? Apple is undeniably a successful organization by the measures of profits and turnover. However, debates over the amount of cash that the company is sitting on and its relationships with shareholders highlight the fact that its strategy is based on security and control. Apple's highly controlled and centralized structure does not play in favor of a savoir-relier mind-set: instead of open communication and sharing, we are more likely to find secrecy and individualism.

Apple certainly is innovative, inventing products that anticipate the needs and dreams of millions of customers and developing marketing strategies that rely on partnerships. The company is also relational and generative, inventing a new sense for society with iPhones, iPads, FaceTime, and other tools that facilitate access to information and connections between people. Apple does influence society and can be argued to have a positive impact on the world. In this sense, Apple is a savoir-relier organization that invents ways to address economic and societal questions. However, generosity and genuineness do not seem to be the company's forte. For example, although it could be argued that the online Apple Store induces ethical behavior by making it easy for people to buy music on the web rather than downloading it illegally, the revenues generated could probably be more equitably shared with musicians and composers, or with the music industry as a whole.

Pascal Cagni pushed for an integrated vision of business where cross-fertilization and sharing among all players would develop new content and ideas. In education, for example, he partnered with European schools, inviting faculty to reflect upon the use of iPads and podcasts in classrooms and develop interactive practices to enhance teaching with the use of Apple servers and products. He also traveled across his region to participate in business reviews that gathered teams of executives to share their experiences and results. These sessions were often tense and difficult, but they were also a great opportunity for open exchanges on whatever issues the company was facing. They were an opportunity to connect across businesses and provide a moment of conviviality, as each review would be followed by an informal dinner. These moments reinforced the participants' sense of belonging to a great company and their desire to help it grow.

Apple was heavily reliant on its charismatic, even iconic CEO, Steve Jobs. But in this well-structured and forward-looking company, Tim Cook had long since been prepared to carry the standard after Jobs's death. The question of sense and identity may need reflection moving forward. Apple's stock price tumbled by a quarter between September 2012 and January 2013 in spite of record results in the first quarter of 2013: 47.8 million iPhones were sold in the last quarter of 2012 and the company recorded average weekly revenue of $4.2 billion compared to $3.3 billion in 2011. Still, investors are in doubt as they see some decelerating revenue growth, declining profit margins, increasing competition, and market saturation.

When revenue growth is accelerating and margins are increasing, investors are often willing to ignore high valuations. But when revenue growth is decelerating and margins are declining, even low valuations sometimes aren't enough to induce investors to buy. Investors don't like downward change because it raises doubt and decreases confidence in the sense that the company is giving to its strategy. They wonder what the company can do to maintain or improve its results. With $135 billion in cash and no debt, the company is clearly well managed and successful. However, the Apple ecosystem is a closed one, meaning the sense of ownership and belonging is therefore very strong: you are Mac or PC. But in a world of open-source software and sharing, the dominance of Apple products could be challenged by freer, more accessible, more versatile options. The company is also facing tough competition and questions about its positioning. With savoir-relier, Apple could find avenues that open the door to a more caring and sharing business while remaining the genius inventor it has been.

Addressing two key questions could open Apple's strategy to savoir-relier: What is our sense of purpose today? How can we give back and share our savoir-faire to improve society's wellbeing? Giving money back to its shareholders may be one step toward opening but it does not really answer those questions. Working on such questions could help restore investors' faith in a future where innovation is combined with influence, confidence, and collaboration or a generative, genuine, and generous organization.

Poilâne: When Quality Nurtures Growth
The context is very different with our third example of a savoir-relier mindset, which concerns a small family business rather than a massive, global corporation. Understanding how Apollonia Poilâne leads her company is

an opportunity to ask more questions about ways to grow business while instilling a culture of transparency, sharing, and innovation.

It may seem easier to instill values across smaller organizations with fewer employees and less diversity, but the question of savoir-relier is not one of size. The courage required to hold on to your values and to stand strong when times are difficult is the same whether you are leading a company with 300,000 employees or 160. Small and large companies alike need the same genuine, generous, and generative skills to generate innovation and change in line with the values and sense of the organization. Savoir-relier is a question of mind-set.

At Poilâne, the organization's identity is based on tradition and quality as well as innovation. For instance, the originality of the company's "kitchen/bar" concept has met great success. Traditionally, French bakeries do not provide a place to sit down and eat, so the addition of a little kitchen/restaurant next to the bakery in the sixth arrondissement of Paris is truly innovative. It is also always full. Customers can enjoy soup or open sandwiches with bacon and cheese or other flavors that enhance the flavor of Poilâne's unique sourdough bread. Poilâne opened the first kitchen bar in 1998; a second one in London met with the same success. Rather than spreading the company thin and developing Poilâne's business by opening more and more bakeries and restaurants, however, Apollonia Poilâne took the time to reflect on her strategy. She wanted to keep on innovating but did not want to fall into the trap of easy but risky mindless expansion.

Positive change is grounded in strong, quality relationships and established trust, along with the energy to develop new ideas. Apollonia Poilâne's goal is to reinforce the unique quality of the Poilâne brand, which has a worldwide reputation anchored in the company's respect for its original manufacturing methods, the environment, and its employees and customers.

In a desire to thrive and maintain quality, Poilâne's leadership is now working on opening a new bakery and shop in Antwerp, Belgium. The modus operandi involves repeated visits to get to know the people, understand their culture, and capture the town's specific character in order to sense if and where a Poilâne bakery will fit in. The time invested in this preparation is time well spent because Apollonia Poilâne wants to build a presence that will be a good fit for the local environment. The Poilâne spirit and positioning should be retained and the company's presence should add value to the area. Poilâne could have launched a very large number of new bakeries and has frequently been solicited to do so in cities like New York. It has chosen not to. Antwerp will be just the third kitchen/bar and bakery to see the light of day.

For some analysts, the current leadership is missing an opportunity to increase profits by pushing for more external growth and rapidly expanding the business. So why isn't Apollonia Poilâne responding to the demands of the market? Her response is that "settling in many cities and imposing Poilâne bakeries on people without serious and mindful reflection partakes of an imperialist culture which is so far from our values. I much prefer taking the time to meet people and build a network of customers who will appreciate our products because they have had a chance to taste them, like them, and trust our quality."[21] Reason and sensibility place quality over quantity and respect over profit. The result is greater risk management and a higher chance of genuine success. It shows how paying attention to people and their environment can drive success with a capacity to help others grow.

Apollonia Poilâne was looking for a manager in London. She interviewed a woman who seemed to offer all the skills she appreciates in a manager: honesty, drive, and an entrepreneurial spirit. The woman told Poilâne up front that she wanted to launch her own business and would do so at some point; she also mentioned that she had plans for a trip to Australia, which meant that she could not start immediately. Rather than finding this off-putting, Poilâne embraced the idea of building a mutually beneficial, healthy relationship based on trust and honesty, which was enough to convince her to recruit the woman. The relationship started on solid ground and is working well, with both parties feeling that they are learning and developing their own skills at the same time that they are growing the company. The human aspect of this story is typical of Poilâne's very human approach to leadership, which is enabling her company to achieve stable, constant, and contained growth under one watchword: sense.

6 THE SAVOIR-RELIER PROTOCOL
How It Works in Practice

The evolution toward a savoir-relier organization implies the development of new skills, capacities, and mind-sets. The savoir-relier protocol facilitates the acquisition of these skills and mind-sets. Unlike traditional tools, which try to measure people by a score or type, the protocol is a process that is founded in introspection and quality human relations. Once again, we see the difference between sense making—the use of measurement tools to analyze existing conditions and draw conclusions based on the assumption, often flawed, that the same conditions will apply in the future—and sense building, in which savoir-relier draws on current reality to project a vision of the future and acknowledges the potential for growth and change with certainty.

The protocol has been used for ten years; feedback from the hundreds of individuals who have participated makes frequent mention of feelings of confidence, trust, and well-being resulting from its use. Our research shows that it has a positive impact on people's leadership.[1] The process also has a positive viral dimension; we have found that executives who experience the savoir-relier protocol usually find it easier to apply in their team or business unit than other leadership concepts, such as quick wins or mentoring programs. Indeed, one of the advantages of the protocol is its flexibility: it can be applied at a pace that matches the availability and needs of the individual and the organization. While measurement-based systems tend to box people into set behaviors, the savoir-relier approach tends to free people and open new avenues for leadership.

HUMANS ARE TOO COMPLEX TO BE MEASURED
Standard Personality Tests Are Blunt Implements

Assessment tools have long invaded the way we think, live, and relate to one another. Because of our obsession with numbers and measurements, we often find that knowing the results of an assessment skews our perception and judgment of the person concerned. A wide range of methodologies is at our disposal to define individuals, from IQ tests of analytical and logical intelligence, to EQ tests of emotional intelligence, and even CQ tests for cultural intelligence. These standardized tests deliver scores or classifications that tell us where we are on a given scale and allow us to compare ourselves, or be compared, with other people. If your IQ score is 150 or above you will forever be classified as a genius; someone who scores around 100 points will be seen as normal and unexceptional. But what do those scores say about your genuine self, about how we change over time, and about our capacity to interact with others?

Some assessment tools, such as the Myers-Briggs Type Indicator and the Insight Inventory, try to measure and categorize personality. They rely on frames of reference, usually drawn from psychological theory. The Myers-Briggs relies on Carl Jung's personality types theory, for example, while the Insight Inventory is based on the work of three theorists: Kurt Lewin, Gordon Allport, and Raymond Cattell. Companies running the assessments often advertise how quick and easy they are to take. Indeed, the assessments are generally done online, using self-administered multiple-choice questionnaires, and are self-scored. At the end, the participant is told which type or profile they match; essentially, they are put into a box, which is categorized according to letters, descriptors, or sometimes colors.

While I am not rejecting the usefulness of psychometric testing and personality profiling, I would warn against paying too much attention to the resulting boxes or set descriptors that are used. After receiving your Myers-Briggs report in a debrief session, you will tend to say, "I am an

ENTJ, and you?" While it is an easy shorthand, the categorization that you are "extrovert, intuitive, thinking, and judging" is also reductive, and there is a risk that you will justify your behaviors on the basis of your assessed type or allow the assessment to lead you to behave in certain ways.

When I underwent Myers-Briggs certification training, I was struck by people's desire to fit in or resemble a type. One member of my group was the only one of his type and he felt like an outsider; people who had been identified as belonging to more common types found comfort in not being singled out. Seemingly, in a group of twenty-four executives in which all but two had been assessed as having a preference for extroversion, the two individuals who had introversion in their type felt estranged. This also affected the group dynamic because of the perception the others had of those two isolated "introverts" even though, in the reality of the exchange within the group, the preference for introversion or extroversion was not so obvious. Indeed, although there are nuances and shades for each type that should be used to temper the diagnosis, once people have been tested or diagnosed, they can't help identifying with their type and often comply with the description provided by the test report.

The complexity of personality is linked to its dynamic and changing nature based on the situation or relationships involved. No one has found a way to discern who you are by computerized or standardized tests alone, simply because the human being is a complex and moving "thing" that cannot be measured. If we accept that it is important and desirable to be genuine, how then should we go about finding our genuine self?

First of all, if you are using tools such as Myers-Briggs, you must analyze their results in the light of your relational experience by discussing types, behaviors, or facets and by challenging the test's conclusions against memories of how you behaved in real-life situations. Putting things into perspective and being prompted to think about your character is always a positive exercise because it raises self-awareness. Also, before you take any such test, it is extremely important to ask yourself three basic but fundamental questions. First, why am I taking this test? Is it to increase my self-awareness or to improve my relationships or for some other reason? Second, what is the contextual use of the test? Is it for my own personal use or for a professional diagnosis? And third (if you are being pushed to take it by your organization), how is my environment going to use the test? Will it be used for personal development or for selection or promotion?

Regardless of the purpose of the test, I argue that the feedback and categorization delivered as a result of answering multiple-choice questionnaires can be dangerous when it is not followed up with thoughtful exchange. I suggest we should move from profiles to portraits.

Profile vs. Portrait

A profile is the side view, outline, or representation of an object or a person; it delineates the contour of the individual. In business, the profile is a formal summary of the distinctive features of a candidate. A portrait, on the other hand, attempts to capture the nuances of its subject and is both more complete and more subtle than a profile. It can be a painting, drawing, sculpture, photograph, or verbal description, like those of characters we find in literature. This is why I choose to refer to the portrait when characterizing a good leader or manager.

If a profile is like a curriculum vitae (CV), a portrait is like the covering letter that explores and explains our capacities in more depth. A portrait requires a different approach from the standard CV outlining the experience and strengths of a person. It implies that the description covers different layers of analysis, again in common with the characterization we find in a novel or play, for instance. A portrait shows the reality of the person without judgment; the smile and the sparkling eyes are offered to the viewer's perception. Think about the famous portrait of the Mona Lisa, *La Joconde*, and all the mystery that surrounds her. In a portrait, the person is telling you something about his or her personality, emotions, feelings, and state of mind and puts you in a position where you can respond. Everything from the expression on the face to the position of the hands gives precise and profound indicators of who the person is.

The portrait goes deeper into the layers of the self as a relational being and builds sense from both positive and difficult parts of our experience. The portrait defines individuals by highlighting their sensible, emotional, spiritual, and rational characteristics for what they are: a reflection of the complex and contradictory nature of the self, one that requires effective self-awareness and introspection.

The Cursor: A Nuanced Approach to Strengths and Weaknesses

In business, people are mostly defined by their strengths and weaknesses as presented in the CVs and covering letters that are the first sources of contact on a very competitive job market. Candidates respond to a job posting by describing their unique profile, which is composed of their education, experience, and interests. The facts they report are meant to highlight personality features that correspond to the job profile. They detail their skills in the covering letter that goes with the CV. If selected for an interview, they will illustrate and explain their perceived strengths and weaknesses at that stage.

Similarly in executive training, leadership programs are often designed to work on the assessed strengths and weaknesses of participants, their good and bad qualities. I argue that we should think differently and recruit and train people by addressing their characteristics and their dynamic, changing nature. A perceived strength can turn out to be a weakness, depending on the situation. I want to present an approach to understanding oneself and others that uses a cursor to reflect the possible movement and evolution of a given characteristic in time and space.

Let's consider a recognized strength in leadership: courage. By using the cursor, we can see how this strength can turn into a weakness, depending on the circumstances. The cursor provides a way of thinking about our characteristics in the light of real-life situations, both personal and professional. It also helps us optimize our actions according to the situation by raising our awareness of the need to adapt our behavior in line with circumstances. The cursor also helps replace bald "good or bad" judgments about characteristics with an understanding of the behavioral response within the setting. It addresses the sense-relational dimension of our personality traits. Let's look at a couple of examples.

Mary is very courageous. This is perceived as a strength by her colleagues and friends. One stormy day on the coast in Brittany she sees a man struggling in the water. Without hesitating, she jumps off a cliff to save him from drowning. However, the swell is so heavy and the currents are so strong that she is beaten back by the sea and has to swim to safety before she needs to be saved herself. She risked her life but wasn't able to rescue the man. In the meantime, Sam, who has a reputation for being fearful, has called the coast guard. The drowning man is saved. With respect to decision making, Sam clearly made a better decision than Mary, even though we would tend to rate "courage" as a strength and "fearfulness" as a weakness. In this case, Mary was too far along the courage spectrum, which meant courage equated to rashness and foolhardiness. Sam, on the other hand, although he lacked courage and remained fearful, compensated for this by relying on other capacities, such as quick-wittedness. The cursor for courage would work as follows:

Coward or cautious?   Courageous or irresponsible?

　　　　Sam   Mary

Webster's dictionary defines *courage* as "mental or moral strength to venture, persevere, and withstand danger, fear, or difficulty."[2]

Let's now consider an organizational situation. An engineer in the company where Sam and Mary work asks both of them to support her idea for a new product in a presentation to their boss. The boss doesn't think the new product will work; the engineer believes in the product and is challenging the boss's authority in the hope that she will be allowed to develop it. Both Mary and Sam know they may fall out of favor with their boss if they side with the engineer. Fearful Sam refuses to stand up. Courageous Mary supports the idea despite the risks and facilitates its implementation even though it goes against the boss's judgment. The product launch is a success but the boss is annoyed by the way they went about it. Sam is still on good terms with his boss but has lost the respect of his colleagues and gets no credit for the new product. Mary and the engineer have developed a successful product but are no longer on good terms with their boss.

There is no right or wrong in Sam and Mary's decisions; anticipating the consequences of different actions or decisions in a specific situation is a way to work on your characteristics and live with them while feeling good about yourself. In fact, Sam had very good reasons not to side with the engineer: a looming promotion, another project for which he needed to remain on good terms with his boss, and the simple fact that he did not believe in the project. Mary made a conscious, self-aware decision to confront her boss and stand behind the engineer despite the risks to her reputation. Each of them is able to assume responsibility for the consequences of their decision. Being aware of where you stand and staying true to yourself will help you understand, accept, and adapt to the decisions you make, and then move on.

Try to picture yourself on this line and visualize your actions. Focus on moments when you felt courageous and tell the story of what happened with details of the decisions you made or actions you took, then place the cursor where your decision puts you. Writing down those moments will help you reflect on your characteristics and understand where you really stand. It will also show you how the cursor shifts to the left or to the right as situations change and as you grow and change over time. Leaders who are very slow at making decisions are sometimes perceived as cowards, while others who make decisions very rapidly can be perceived as irresponsible. The important thing to remember is the relational aspect of the situation and that other people's judgment of your behavior is subjective and will be informed by where their own cursor lies.

Characteristics such as courage and fear can and do evolve over time. An awareness of this is useful to leaders who build on self-awareness and mindfulness by relying on the relationships and the sense involved in a particular situation. In the drowning man example given earlier, fear becomes wisdom if the currents are so strong that they risk dragging you under. The cursor can help us temper our instincts in the face of a real-life situation. The same cursor applies to any perceived strength or weakness. Presented in the right light or in the right situation, almost any characteristic can be seen in a positive or a negative light. For instance, adaptability, which is generally perceived to be a strength, can turn someone into a "chameleon" who melds with her environment and has a hard time standing up for herself and what she believes. Equally, determination, another perceived strength, can lead to extreme stubbornness and a refusal to take advice or listen to others. There is no right or wrong in being who you are, but you need to know where you stand to be yourself.

By working with the cursor and understanding your characteristics and how you operate, you will grow your confidence in your capacity to make better decisions. Rather than having a mental checklist of strengths and weaknesses, you will have a more genuine sense of who you are as a whole person. Tools to grow self-awareness prove effective when you are capable of acknowledging your limitations. The process of self-awareness will allow you to find out where you stand and how your responses change as the world changes around you. Self-awareness is a source of confidence: the confidence to accept your imperfections and incompleteness, the confidence to listen and adapt to the needs of others and inspire trust.

EXPLORING THE SAVOIR-RELIER PROTOCOL
The ACE Learning Strategy

Leadership involves a set of cognitive, social, political, psychological, and moral talents and skills, all of which can be enhanced with the right training. As we will see, the savoir-relier protocol uses a learning strategy called ACE, which stands for analytical, critical, and experiential. The protocol uses an analytical phase to build knowledge and theory, a critical dimension to increase self-awareness and bring a global perspective to the learning experience, and an experiential component so participants practice certain skills. The method focuses on the capacity to forge critical connections between the theory of savoir-relier and its application in order to understand it and adapt it to diverse cultures. It helps leaders establish constructive links between knowledge and skills so as to effectively train people to manage the complexity of relationships.

Combined with work on the individual, interpersonal, organizational, and institutional dimensions of savoir-relier, the ACE learning strategy helps participants learn and practice skills and uncover and develop their capacities. It has proved to be very effective in many different settings: the balance of theory, practice, and self-reflection creates conditions for learning that cover all four levels of development and provide a complete understanding of your leadership skills.

The Protocol and the Principles of Relationality

The savoir-relier protocol applies the four principles of relationality—perception, reliance, resilience, and responsibility—to identify and grow the skills needed to become a sense-relational being. Savoir-relier leaders are not extraterrestrials who are born with unique capacities. The skills and capacities they have can be learned by anyone who has the will to learn and the desire to play a role in society. It is intended for anyone who is not driven by the sole purpose of making money, whose motivation is not simply to acquire power and increase profits. Anyone can become a sense-relational being and grow effective leadership skills to face difficult, uncertain, and complex environments. Some develop the skills attached to those principles naturally, without even knowing it, while others need to enhance their capacity to perceive, their self-awareness, and their resilience or sense of responsibility. But skills are one thing; what you do with them is really what matters. Sometimes life forces us to acquire those skills; at other times, we make a conscious decision to draw out those skills to equip ourselves to handle complexity.

The example of Clara Gaymard is a case in point. Her leadership skills align with the four principles of relationality. Her sensibility and perception grew with looking after her nine children, listening attentively to them, and making use of all her senses to provide the care each child needed. Reliance was critical to build a sense of trust with each child and to provide a warm environment for the children to get along with and rely on each other. The level of cohesion, respect, and understanding between those kids has always amazed me. Then, because life is never a smooth ride, and educating nine kids comes with hardship, Gaymard developed resilience. For Gaymard, staying strong when her son was on the brink of dying while her daughter sat next to her in the taxi was a key moment that demonstrated her resilience and changed her perception of herself as a resilient person.

Finally, her sense of responsibility has been shared and built on the trust that every individual in her family has a place, a role, and a responsibility to contributing to the wellness of the others. Early on, each of Gaymard's children learned to be responsible for themselves and for their brothers and sisters, sharing responsibility in their individual roles while Gaymard and her husband were assuming their roles as parents and as business or political leaders in parallel with their responsibilities as guiding and caring parents and role models.

What Gaymard developed naturally through her experience and role as a mother raising a large family while pursuing a career as a leader, others can develop by exercising each of the four relationality principles within the savoir-relier protocol. I designed this protocol as part of a leadership curriculum that would help my students at HEC become more self-aware and better able to relate to others. The four principles are central to this process of building awareness, confidence, trust, resilience, and a true sense of purpose and responsibility.

Let's see how the protocol can be implemented in leadership development seminars or used as a means to support an individual who decides to work on his or her leadership capacities. The protocol does not require a qualification in coaching or a PhD in psychology; anyone who understands the value of interpersonal exchange and agrees that improving the quality of our relationships can improve the well-being of all will find the savoir-relier protocol beneficial.

Once you understand the goal of savoir-relier, the process is easy to follow. However, you need to be prepared and willing to step outside your comfort zone, which is not easy for everyone. To make the most of the experience, you need a strong will and the determination to look into the mirror of the self.

Using the Protocol to Drive Individual and Collective Well-Being
Working on the sensible and intuitive sides of leadership requires hard work and intense energy. It means delving into unusual and sometimes uncomfortable areas that touch on the private, intimate side of the self. The result is an increased capacity to address complex problems and greater self-awareness, both of which build confidence. Interpersonal exchange, which is a key part of the process, brings insights into our capacity to build effective relationships with the other. Following the savoir-relier protocol also grows our capacity to listen and receive feedback on personal, emotional, spiritual, sensible, and sometimes sensitive issues. The moment of exchange reveals the value of simple, direct, and genuine talk to grow the interpersonal skills that condition effective management practices. You will be guided to address your contradictions and seek your true identity by working on resilience. Finally, you will engage in decentering and driving positive change by uncovering your creative self.

The applied objective of the savoir-relier protocol is to unfold your ability to engage in qualitative interaction with others and transfer this capacity to your operational leadership actions. I will detail how the work on perception, reliance, and resilience helps us to engage with others and lead them toward action and innovation based on shared goals and shared responsibility and, of course, to generate sense.

METHODOLOGY AND IMPACT OF THE SAVOIR-RELIER PROTOCOL

Understanding the Methodology

To begin the protocol you need to adopt an attitude of openness to reflection and sharing. In a leadership development seminar, this means that the selected participants must agree to commit to the process, which has been approved and supported by the management of the company. There is no right or wrong way of acting or speaking at any given moment in the protocol. The content and output are risk free and respectful of the values and culture of the individual participants and of the organization. The only requirement is that participants are willing to step out of their comfort zone and experiment with new ways of thinking and doing.

As we saw earlier, the methodology is based on the ACE approach, which combines analytical, critical, and experiential learning. The perceived positive value of qualitative, sensible, and personal exchange from the savoir-relier protocol brings a sense of confidence and trust that makes people feel good. The trust established between the members of the group through the medium of interpersonal exchange opens the door for work on difficult areas and an analysis of resilience and agility mechanisms for each individual.

Building on the individual characteristics identified during the initial phases of the protocol, the group draws collective conclusions and proposes individual actions based on the understanding of the company's values and identity, its culture and history, and its current challenges within the wider business context. The result is an understanding of the potential for change and innovation within the framework established by the corporate identity and culture. The savoir-relier protocol offers new ways for a company to value individual specificities and the quality of interpersonal skills to enhance a collective identity that is coherent and compatible with individuals' personalities, aspirations, and desires.

The protocol combines writing, oral, and interactive exercises with observation and actions that draw on individual, introspective, interpersonal, organizational, and global perspectives. It addresses both personal and professional issues as a basis for interpersonal exchange and deals with both positive and negative experiences.

When used in an organizational setting, the savoir-relier approach requires three conditions to be effective. First, the size of the group should be limited to twenty-four participants if possible and should not exceed thirty. It is important for the seminar to have enough participants for a good group dynamic to develop but to leave enough space for individual expression. Because the protocol involves one-on-one interaction with the sharing of self-portraits, an even number of participants is recommended.

Second, participants should be representative of the diversity that exists in the organization in terms of function, nationality, gender, experience, and so forth. Diversity makes an important contribution to stimulating exchange and intensive interpersonal work. It is also a good way to capture the value of differences and to experience perception across boundaries. For example, men and women often interpret self-portraits in different lights, while a junior manager sharing his or her perception of a senior executive will open avenues that resonate differently from the discussion that will ensue when two senior executives exchange opinions.

Third, key challenges or sources of tensions for the group should be identified. This condition is the source of collective work and group identity. The challenges or tensions chosen must be current, serious, and real. They provide material for the participants to test the skills that are revealed by the early stages of the protocol and are a fast and effective way to measure their impact. The challenges, whether they relate to the launch of a new product or cost-cutting measures, will be used to help each team identify leadership actions that engage each individual's responsibility.

Implementing the Protocol: A Four-Stage Transformative Process
When times are tough, people tend to center on themselves to protect their interests and acquired benefits or privileges. Savoir-relier facilitates

contact in an easy, healthy, and simple way; all you need is to be willing to share. The savoir-relier protocol can be implemented in a wide range of settings including corporate seminars for personal and leadership development; management programs like the MBA, EMBA, or Master of Science in Management; or courses involving communication and personal development. Individuals who wish to develop their leadership skills on their own can also use the protocol.

The protocol has four stages plus a preparatory stage, each of which can function separately or as a complete cycle. Each stage addresses individual and collective roles, performance, and identity. We will begin by looking at the preparatory stage for a savoir-relier seminar: the writing of a self-portrait, which will be used in Stage 2 of the protocol.

Preparatory Stage: The Self-Portrait Technique: A Process of Self-Awareness. In *An Intimate History of Humanity*, the British philosopher and historian Theodore Zeldin places portraits of living people and historical figures side by side and discusses the lessons we can learn from the comparison.[3] He explores how humans have lost hope and how encounters have revived them; how men and women have learned to have interesting conversations; how some people have acquired an immunity to loneliness; how new forms of love have been invented; how respect has become more desirable than power; how those who want neither to give orders nor to receive them can become intermediaries; why even the privileged are often gloomy; and how people choose a way of life only to find it does not wholly satisfy them.

While working with Zeldin on ways to transform management education in 2003, we decided to experiment with the conversation approach in the HEC MBA curriculum. Savoir-relier had proved to be a powerful tool to reform the structure of the MBA program, and the highly collaborative, diverse group of students who were in the program at the time were actively engaging in the transformation process. I offered the students an opportunity to engage in self- and interpersonal reflection during the program through the use of self-portraits. Zeldin and I developed forty questions to guide their introspection. The questions were designed to promote introspection and open the students' eyes to a wider understanding of how they related to others and their environment.

Zeldin created a "menu of conversation" that was distributed to participants, who paired up over lunch or dinner and used the questions on the menu to spark a discussion. After a few years of experimentation with the self-portrait, I decided to channel the process of self-awareness through four levels or layers of understanding to reflect the four dimensions of relational leadership: you and yourself—the individual level; you and others—the interpersonal level; you and your group, organization, or team—the organizational level; and you and society—the institutional or societal level.

There are ten questions for each level, some of which are drawn from Zeldin's original work. Examples of questions include the following: "What are your fears and have they diminished, increased, or changed with the passing years?" "What are the limits of your compassion?" "In which domains do you wish to lead? In which domains do you wish to follow?" "How do you usually behave in work teams?"

Each level involves dimensions of relationships or principles of relationality that stimulate the participants' thoughts, preoccupations, concerns, and interests at the specific moment of reflection and writing. This is an important point because it means that a self-portrait is not fixed in time. Indeed, different portraits can be written at different moments in your life and reveal different aspects of yourself and your relationships each time. Each portrait is like a photograph of yourself at a given moment. Introspection is a means to enhance self-awareness or self-reliance. The act of writing is critical in the process as it leaves a trace that materializes impressions, feelings, emotions, and perceptions as words.

The self-portrait is a free-writing exercise. The questions are designed to guide participants' initial thoughts and drive their responses in note form. Each participant chooses to address three or four questions for each layer of analysis and write down their spontaneous thoughts and ideas. The notes serve as a base on which to write a self-portrait that is a narrative of self, a story in a cursive form. Some people choose to put more emphasis on some layers of analysis than others; these are indicators of the dominant concerns at a given time in their life. Some people find they struggle with self-discovery and understanding at a time of personal growth, while others might emphasize their relationship to society at a later stage of their life and career. People's relationships with their organization and those around them also fluctuate over time. For example, the organizational relationship might dominate the self-portrait at important moments like a change in career or a promotion, while interpersonal relationships will come to the fore at times of personal stress or happiness.

Feedback on the writing process itself reveals different impressions: "challenging but useful," "smooth and comforting," "enlightening," and "difficult but telling" are the kinds of comments that frequently emerge following the self-portrait experience. People who think that they have already done similar introspective work often change their mind after participating in the self-portrait exercise. The elements that differentiate the self-portrait from other exercises in introspection are the four levels of reflection, the open guiding questions that touch on both personal and professional sides of life, and the fact that it is a free-writing exercise.

Writing a self-portrait can take anything from one hour to eight hours and can be spread over several days. On some occasions a person who has a vital need for self-analysis may spend more than eight hours and rework his or her self-portrait after a savoir-relier workshop or seminar. After the seminar, people often report back that they have chosen to use the self-portrait with their partner or spouse to improve the quality of their relationship. As well as being a free-writing and free-sharing exercise, the self-portrait provides a strong base from which to grow the perception and sensibility that we go on to explore in the first stage of the protocol.

Stage 1: Perception and Sensibility.   The first stage of the protocol involves work on a combined rational, emotional, spiritual, and sensible approach to tackle complex problems. It relies on exercises to develop true sensibility and dissociate interpretation from sensation in our relationships with our environment. It also creates an awareness and understanding of the value of the primary senses in refining our perception of the world around us and our individual capacity to engage in interpersonal exchange at an intimate level, even in a professional setting.

A wide range of exercises are used during this first stage. These include such things as sessions describing paintings to clarify the difference between what you "see" versus what you "think" and what you "feel," and wine or food tastings that raise awareness of sensory perception. The ultimate aim of this first stage is to connect to our senses and understand the role of perception versus analysis versus emotions in our relationship to the world and people around us. It prepares the ground for the second stage, where awareness, introspection, and receptivity are critical.

In seminars that aim to complete the full protocol cycle, the goals to be achieved in this first stage also include the identification of tensions or challenges that justify the presence of the group. Each individual is offered a chance to express his or her role in the organization and in relation to the identified challenge. Examples of challenges include a desire for more innovation or expanded cross-functional teamwork and a need for improved crisis or change management in the context of a restructuring plan or acquisition. The challenge that is identified is a testing ground where participants can exercise their newly acquired sense-relational skills directly and test the impact of confidence, trust, resilience, and sense building on decision making and responsible acts of leadership. The relational circuit serves as a model to unfold the challenge and propose pioneering approaches to existing business.

Stage 2: Developing Reliance with Self-Portraits and Conversation. Having worked to enhance their capacity for perception in Stage 1, the participants move on to work on interpersonal reliance with a view to developing confidence and trust. There are three steps in this important phase. The first is the preparatory phase, which was completed before Stage 1: the writing of the self-portrait. The second step is to discuss the self-portrait with another member of the group in a conversation. The third step is to unfold and discuss the perceived characteristics of our self-portrait conversation partner based on their self-portrait and the ensuing exchange. The person with whom we share our self-portrait has gone through the same process of reflection and has written a similar document.

The fact that both individuals in the conversation have done the same introspective work and have before them a page or two of writing that mirrors their genuine image is critical. The act of exchanging self-portraits is a way to exert our generosity. The face-to-face conversation that follows this exchange is a moment of sharing and giving where our attention is focused on the other. Participants listen, give feedback, and question each other in a moment of equality and reciprocity. The exchange is an exercise in perception and reliance.

With this second step, the objective is to engage in genuine, generous, and generative conversation where you learn to speak candidly and receive and give feedback that is acute, sensible, and constructive. Sometimes the conversation takes place between two perfect strangers, sometimes between direct reports or colleagues. The pairings vary depending on the group's interests and situation. The conversations can be useful in a personal setting as well, taking place between friends, spouses, partners, or relatives. Each member of the pairing needs to read his or her partner's self-portrait before the conversation takes place.

The setting for the conversation requires face-to-face space with some privacy. Even so, multiple conversations can take place simultaneously in the same room simply because people's concentration is incredibly intense once the conversation has begun. An important point is to make sure there is enough time scheduled for a quality exchange. Two hours is generally felt to be a good amount of time.

The format of the conversation should allow equal time to each member and respect the following rules:

- Speak freely about any issues you feel comfortable to share.
- Focus on moments, events, or memories.
- Remain open to feedback and questions.
- Be perceptive, candid, and constructive in your feedback: acknowledge your subjectivity.
- Let the conversation flow.
- Avoid judgment or drawing conclusions.

To break the ice, the conversation starts with each speaker explaining which of the forty questions they chose to address for their self-portrait and why. This helps participants to jump straight to the heart of the matter. From there, the exchange, sharing, common interests, and discussions tend to flow naturally. At the end of the two hours, each participant writes down two characteristics—sharp, direct, shy, humble, self-assured, low self-esteem, and so on—that he or she believes describe himself or herself, and two that describe the other person. The peers then swap their four words and compare the results. They discuss the reasons behind their choice and explain the differences or similarities in their perceptions.

When done as part of a seminar, the conversations are followed by a debriefing session on the notion of characteristics versus strengths and weaknesses, with reference to the characteristics perceived during the conversation. The debriefing serves as a transition to the next stage. Every time I run a conversation session, the pairs find that "time was too short," even when the idea of spending two hours talking seemed an eternity or "time wasted" for some before doing it. The conversation exercise reveals the value of "the other" as a person with sensibility. Because perception is reality—the reality as seen, felt, and thought by an individual—the person who has read your self-portrait and listened to you acts as a mirror and helps you see yourself more clearly in the reflection. As a result, having several conversations of the same kind with different people keeps enriching your self-awareness while developing your capacity to be truly involved with another.

The benefits of such quality and trustworthy moments of exchange are undeniable and unanimous. Some see "a moment of truth" or "a revelation," or declare that they spoke about things that they had never shared before with anyone, not even a best friend or parent. Others mention "the value of time spent on such quality moments" and "confidence in the other person," or say they feel better about their capacity to speak up. They "appreciate the genuine feedback" or highlight how it feels "to know what someone else really thinks about you." Even those who are skeptical about the assignment beforehand admit that they are "amazed by the power of such simple exercise" and wish they could spend more time doing more of this.

As discussed previously, time is an important factor in our ability to manage and lead in complex environments. The conversation is an exercise in trust and openness but also an exercise in setting aside time for quality interaction. It highlights the fact that it is up to each individual to decide how to allocate his or her time. Following this experience, some executives have decided to replace a number of the long and repetitive meetings that most companies hold every week with conversation moments, asking members of their team to engage in conversation using savoir-relier protocol questions in place of a formal meeting. Feedback indicates that this approach has a positive impact on the quality of teamwork and interpersonal relationships: "it strengthens bonds across groups of people," "a team that was experiencing conflicts started working together with understanding," "it facilitated the sharing of creative and spontaneous ideas, which are often the source of innovation." The impact of conversation can go beyond expectations and generate new business for companies.

Stage 3: Resilience Mechanisms Drawn from Real-Life Experience.   The third stage of the protocol focuses on individual resilience and participants' ability to transfer resilience mechanisms into live situations. This step builds on the knowledge, confidence, and trust acquired during previous stages. Participants apply their enhanced sensible awareness to difficult decision-making, communication, and people management processes. They learn to revisit real-life experiences of difficult situations and assess how they functioned. They explore the techniques they have used in the past to manage challenging operational situations relating to performance management, conflict resolution, or crisis situations. Story-telling and direct feedback are used to explore the kinds of resilience that they found within themselves.

With a genuine assessment of your experience and a better understanding of your capacity for resilience, you are better prepared to address present or possible crisis management and communication settings. If your organization is facing a crisis or challenge, or if you are facing a personal conflict or problem, the exercises in the protocol can be applied directly to the situation. In other cases, projection and external situations can be used.

In the context of a leadership seminar, the session on resilience is an opportunity to test your agility; your capacity to question, adapt, and change your behavior; and your ability to respond with confidence in a group setting. It tests your personality and personal characteristics by obliging you to address a challenging problem. At one seminar, for example, Pat, an executive director in a telecom company, told the story of the last time he had fired one of his employees. Pat spoke about how he had prepared himself for the moment with all the right arguments and described his calm, self-controlled demeanor when the employee walked into his office.

Using disjunctive analysis, Pat revealed how his self-control was, in fact, only a superficial way of masking his fears. In the heat of the moment his anxiety betrayed him and the employee left his office upset and angry because, on top of being fired, he did not feel respected. We applied the relational circuit to understand the mechanisms of Pat's resilience. He needed to work on building a more genuine attitude so that when similar situations arose in the future, he would not appear as a cold-blooded, irresponsible boss but as the concerned, empathetic person he really is.

Projecting yourself into a new and unknown situation requires agility; it requires a subtle balance between structure and improvisation. Confidence, risk, letting go, and trial and error are all ways to practice and enhance your resilience and agility. But only if you are willing to learn. You must learn to speak about your experiences and decode your reactions to them, learn to challenge yourself, experiment with new ways of relating to people, and push your limits while staying true to your values and those of your organization.

In the full cycle of the savoir-relier seminar, a session on resilience and agility is organized around sports and the leadership scorecard. Participants are offered an opportunity to test their abilities by engaging in individual and team sports, supervised by professional coaches and observed by their peers. Scorecards are used to analyze and decode the behaviors and attitudes that people demonstrate in three areas: physical and sensorial, emotional, and moral. Each area has key words that correspond to certain behaviors, and the behaviors are associated with certain scores. Different individuals score your performance at different times. They then share their observations with you in the form of a feedback and discussion session, and you do the same thing for others.

This session is a fantastic opportunity to understand the impact of stress, fear, agility, sharing, and openness on your behavior in active settings. The goal is to absorb the observations and feedback and relate the findings to your story of resilience. Then, by applying the relational circuit, you can work on decentering as the last stage of the protocol unfolds.

Stage 4: Leadership Actions to Grow Responsibility and Sense. The fourth stage of the savoir-relier protocol binds perception, reliance, and resilience with responsibility and, of course, sense. Sense is where resilience and agility operate their magic; sense reconciles the interests of the individual with those of the organization. Sense is how the relational circuit can be used to address challenges through work on best practices and leadership actions that have genuine impact and influence. Sense is the key to improving your performance by developing leadership initiatives that respond to the corporate challenges you are facing today.

The purpose of this final stage is twofold: to highlight your sense of responsibility, and to share and debate possible solutions to problems or work up ideas for innovation. The relational circuit enables you to understand your problems as a whole by analyzing each component and unfolding the relationships that connect the different objects, situations, or people in question. From the resulting relational assimilation you can "decenter" the problem toward the new solution and recreate sense, not only for the parts involved but also for the whole group or organization. The crucial moment of responsibility is in the act of decentering and the following re-creation of sense.

This final stage of the savoir-relier protocol ends the cycle of re-creation by putting you in action. This is the moment when you reconcile your actions with your understanding of yourself, others, and the world around you. It is a moment of responsibility. By analyzing the distance that separated you from your actions and experiences, you have grown a capacity to see new relationships, to understand the expectations or aspirations of your colleagues and subordinates, and to accept the point of view of those around you. You are now able to build sense from your observations and analyses; you are now ready to act. Sense is built in action. It is the result of understanding, judgment, and engagement. The savoir-relier protocol facilitates the emergence of sense because it gives you an opportunity to experiment, test yourself, and learn about yourself and how you relate to others and your environment.

By this stage you are ready to engage in effective and concrete leadership actions and can present your plan to an audience by detailing short-term and long-term actions that reveal the transformation process engaged. Transformation achieved through this process of perception, reliance, resilience, and responsibility is the primary outcome of the savoir-relier protocol. It begins with individual transformation, and it relies on your capacity to work from inner contradictions or tensions. But it also affects your environment, your organization, and the people around you thanks to the relational dimension involved.

Understanding How a Real-Life Seminar Works.   An example of a full cycle of the savoir-relier seminar illustrates how this all works in practice. Some companies choose to use only part of the protocol and focus on specific areas, such as resilience, or the self-portrait and conversation experience. For greater impact, however, particularly at a corporate level when there is a desire to achieve significant improvements in leadership mind-sets across the organization, I recommend the complete cycle. Ideally, four days should be set aside to cover all the material, but it is possible to condense the key elements into two or three days, or even integrate half-day sessions into a larger leadership development seminar with corporate presentations and external speakers. Even though the condensed versions miss out on some of the activities, the value of the savoir-relier experience remains as a seed that will keep on growing.

Here is an example of the format for twenty-four to forty participants with the full cycle over four days:

Day 1: "Savoir-Relier" and Your Corporate Leadership Challenge

- Introduction: complexity management, tensions and paradoxes, relational leadership, agility, and sense of purpose.
- Identification of a challenge in the transformation context of the company: culture, leadership model, innovation processes, restructuration, merger or acquisition, talent management, and so on.
- Experiencing "sense leadership" and the savoir-relier approach: exercise in listening, exercise in observing a painting, exercise in giving feedback.
- Writing of self-portrait.

Lunch: Blind tasting—develop your senses of taste, smell, and touch.

- Sharing self-portraits through conversation and discussion of personality traits.
- Presentation of identified challenges to management or group: dialogue and communication.

Dinner: Food and wine tasting to further explore the senses.

Day 2: Your Personal Leadership Style: The Leadership Scorecard

- Your leadership style in action. The leadership scorecard exercise: outdoor sports if possible, with the participation of professional sports coaches. Exercising, testing, and observing agility, resilience, poise, management control, stress resistance, team spirit, and ethics in action, using a variety of individual and team sports.
- Impact of scorecards: physical and sensory, emotional, moral, and analytical. Understanding what your performance says about your behavior in business leadership contexts.

Lunch: The athlete's diet and health management. Hosted by guest athletes.

- Implications of scorecard results on management capacity: recruitment, performance management, and so on. Analysis of scorecards: feedback from observation.
- Finding your own agility and resilience mechanisms.
- Preparing leadership action plans in teams.

Dinner: Music game based on listening and singing.

Day 3: Crisis Management, Innovation, and Communication

- Understanding crisis and innovation management processes on the basis of the identified challenge, using the relational circuit through role plays.
- Live case studies: innovation and crisis management, prepared before the seminar on the basis of real situations.

Lunch: Food from different cultures; observing chefs and helping prepare snacks in teams.

- Effective communication preparation: cross-cultural awareness, communication style, TED Talk analysis. Individual and team presentations.

Dinner: Full meal prepared by teams.

Day 4: Leadership Actions

- Individual projection of problem resolution in teams: responsibility, relationships, and so on.
- Group reconstruction of the challenge and its leadership implications: relational circuit.

Lunch: Open dialogue/feedback.

- Presentations of initiatives to be implemented in the short and medium term both individually and collectively. What is your sense of purpose? How does your individual sense of purpose fit with the organization's sense of purpose? Option to invite top management to the presentation session.

Farewell cocktail: distribution of savoir-relier certificates and closing session with management.

The benefits of the protocol are numerous, particularly in terms of resolving tensions and contradictions both for individuals and for the company.

Benefits for the Individual

- Understand the importance of genuine talk, active listening, and sensing.
- Discover the value of introspection as a builder of self-awareness and self-confidence.
- Develop a capacity to give and receive feedback thanks to effective introspection.
- Discover the value of one-on-one interpersonal exchange as a source of positive relationships and trust building.
- Develop an understanding of personal resilience mechanisms and their impact on decision-making processes and actions.
- Understand the connections between personal characteristics, corporate values, and sense of purpose.

- Develop crisis management and effective communication behaviors and processes.
- Share best practices with regard to leadership impact on motivation, engagement, change, and restructuring.
- Create leadership action plans for each individual and the group.

Benefits for the Organization

- Develop the human dimension in leadership teams.
- Help executives feel more confident as leaders.
- Train executives as mentors for their teams.
- Grow awareness of collective identity and sense of purpose.
- Increase the energy devoted to people management.
- Create leadership action plans for each division.
- Create new and specific people management and development tools: interviews, mentoring, training, and so on.
- Improve and adapt job-grading processes in a restructuring phase.
- Develop specific and applied leadership actions to improve performance.

From Contradictions to Resolutions

The savoir-relier protocol is founded on the understanding that human beings are complex, living organisms full of contradictions. One way of dealing with our contradictions is to focus only on the bright and positive side of who we are. Positivism has indeed proved successful in stimulating the energy necessary to build and create. However, when difficult situations or crises occur, a positive attitude is not always enough to carry us over the mountain of problems ahead of us.

I have found that those who dig deeper into the darker sides of their being come out stronger in times of crisis. These hidden sides of us conflict with our more comfortable, positive side. This is why we must look at, recognize, and understand our contradictions, our conflicting selves. Ask yourself a simple question: how often do you look at yourself in the mirror? Once or twice a day perhaps, when you put on makeup or shave or brush your teeth. And how deep is that look? It is a superficial look.

So what does your face look like when you are angry or sad or laughing? You don't know, unless there is a photograph of you taken at that precise moment. Only people who see us daily in such moments where we express and show who we truly are can answer this question.

Learning from our contradictions is a way to dive into our portrait with all of its facets, bright and dark, sweet and bitter, soft and hard, without complacency. Dialectics is the logic of change, where things are understood by their internal change and their relationships with other objects. The nature of contradiction is universal, as in life and death, but it is also personal, and each individual is inhabited by specific contradictions. These contradictions are the source of our transformation. This dialectic involves strong ideological context, but it applies to the savoir-relier approach because of the tensions that relationships unveil, whether they oppose order and disorder or structure and sensibility. Those tensions are the source of balance and creativity. We live with our contradictions because they motivate our transformation and define our identity. Let us now see the impact of such an approach on management practices and corporate identity.

Results and Impact
One of the practical outputs of the savoir-relier protocol is a mentoring capacity for those who engage in the learning process. Mentoring becomes a responsibility to be truly engaged with the people around you. It demands that you listen and look for signals that will help you to understand and adapt to the needs of employees or customers and build an environment that favors innovation, performance, and well-being through autonomy and a collaborative structure. The simple notion of care and attention builds confidence in people who then become more active and creative and inclined to go above and beyond the tasks that are assigned to them.

Another practical output is in team management: some executives now organize their performance review system differently thanks to the savoir-relier experience. By introducing conversations as part of their management practices, these executives report an increased awareness of where people stand and much more productive and effective performance reviews. Here is just one example of feedback from an executive in a high-tech company: "The performance review process is no longer perceived as a mechanical 'objectives versus results' exercise. It is a true moment of exchange and an opportunity to share that goes beyond results and targets greater achievements. People appreciate the moment and feel they are respected. They leave more motivated." Individual respect and care have boosted performance.

Another example was reported to me by the CEO of a business unit within a large organization. He decided to use one meeting per month as a conversation meeting, applying the savoir-relier self-portrait and conversation approach. He found that the team started interacting spontaneously, generating ideas and building a much more enthusiastic atmosphere in the office in spite of difficult times.

In my experience running the self-portrait exercise with hundreds of students and executives over the last ten years, every single individual has found the experience to be stimulating, worthwhile, and positive. Reported benefits include greater confidence, increased self-awareness, and, more importantly, "the value of discovering someone else in greater depth" and "the importance of quality attention and interaction."

The desire to invest more in these quality moments is but one positive impact of the protocol at its early stage. The simplicity of its implementation makes the self-portrait and conversation experience a unique tool for individuals, companies, groups, teams, and leaders who want to grow confidence and trust. The rest of the protocol unfolds more practical benefits, such as improved collaboration, innovation, and influence and enhanced individual and organizational performance.

The benefits and repercussions can also be very specific. For example, Jane, who was head of HR in a U.S. business unit, and Tim, who was CEO of a business unit in China, found themselves face to face in a self-portrait conversation session. Tim was facing major recruitment issues in his business unit because of high staff turnover and what seemed like the company's inability to retain talent. During the exchange of personal and professional stories that took place within the conversation session, Tim and Jane discovered that they had lived very different lives: Tim's life had been smooth and eventless compared to Jane's tumultuous history. Tim was very adaptable and had worked in seven different countries, while

Jane had never left the United States. Her interest in people and her love for the job she had been doing for the last eleven years were everything to her. Tim was fascinated by Jane's stories of helping people move, develop, and change careers. He realized the importance of the human aspect in the workplace. Jane helped him hire three people from her network who went on to play a key role in stabilizing his teams in Shanghai and improving work conditions and performance as people started to develop a genuine sense of collaboration.

Of course, tensions remain. The protocol does not resolve difficulties instantly or definitively, but savoir-relier plants the seeds of change. When the seeds grow, people feel more competent and confident, and as more people are touched, there is a positive viral effect. From the need to facilitate quality relationships to the resilience and agility gained in the process, savoir-relier creates sense that is the link between the individual and the group, the organization and society. The magic is that it starts with one person relating to another person, then another, and so on, with a snowball effect on the mind-set of the organization: people talk to each other, smile at each other, say hello, and behave more kindly toward each other. A move in this direction enables us all to live better lives while respecting and valuing our contradictions, our tensions, or, simply, our differences.

Moving to Action
A leader creates himself or herself step by step, over time, through gestures and acts of self-construction in relation to others. By exploring what divides or creates distance between individuals, we come to know ourselves and become more agile. The wider the division, the greater the effort needed to understand the other, and the more agility and self-knowledge is gained in the task of understanding. Interpersonal connections and common ground emerge along the way. These efforts enable us to build the confidence needed to exercise leadership as a process of influence with composure. This capacity is a major step toward exercising responsible, people-centered leadership that is driven by a common purpose and the desire to build sense for them and for the organization.

Our sense-relational approach to leadership builds on the value of developing one's personality, skills, and talents with sense and sensibility. It relies on the capacity to work on one's self first, then to work with another person, then another, and so on in a dynamic process. With confidence, the leader is capable of inspiring trust in others and leveraging trust to build resilience and responsibility at different stages and in different places. Savoir-relier grows organically.

The paradox of leadership is evident in organizations. On one hand, employees are asked to be responsible, autonomous, and creative. On the other hand, too many companies fail to provide employees with the means for personal growth and well-being: corporate cultures are usually strong and rigid and do not have space for individuals who deviate from the norm. As a result, the reign of the unspoken code, of restricted information, of dissimulation, and of artificial human relations persists. Savoir-relier can be seen as part of the solution. It introduces more respect and intelligence to human relationships while liberating individuals, both managers and employees, to be genuine, generous, and generative.

To spread this savoir-relier approach in a sustainable way, leaders will have to accept that they are unable to control everything. They will also need to take advantage of complexity by building relationships across differences and growing an ability to remain open, in a form of serene availability of the type demonstrated by Marissa Mayer when she worked at Google. This source of cohesion lets each individual find his or her place and work toward a common purpose.

The leadership training undertaken in savoir-relier seminars is a quest for meaning, for that sense of purpose that must come from within and light the way for others. The aim is to reconcile individual personalities with the corporate identity through interpersonal relationships. Understanding the company's sense of purpose, which is an expression of the corporate identity, culture, and values, is a necessary step, but it is not sufficient. Each member of the organization needs to accept this sense of purpose and adhere to it in order to move in the same direction together. This requires individual commitment, group cohesion, and agility across the board. Instead, companies often face tension between the agility required to reconcile individual, group, and collective agendas and the indispensable sense of purpose that drives the firm forward but is not naturally aligned with the needs of the individual.

Humility and a form of self-effacement, in place of the more egocentric charismatic leadership models, also mark this leadership insight. Yet adopting this approach is not easy. Developing savoir-relier requires skills and attributes that are often lacking in our societies and organizations, particularly the attribute of courage. Savoir-relier leaders need to have the courage to support others, make tough decisions, tell the truth, and embrace complexity and differences to build organizations where rationality walks side by side with sense. They need to restore common sense, creativity, and sensibility as inherent components of sustainable growth.

7   TRANSLATING POETRY
A Metaphor for Leading in Complex Times

The first course I taught at HEC was American Poetry. Students perceived the course as a great way to practice their English-language skills while expanding their knowledge of American history and culture. Intense class discussions and debates emerged from the complex issues raised in the different poems that we studied. But the thing the students appreciated most was the opportunity the class offered to dive into self-awareness and presence, two essential skills for future leaders. Students engaged in the act of writing and reading poems out loud, using diverse techniques to develop introspection and self-expression, and gained confidence by performing their own work in front of their peers. Using poetry to work on self-awareness, voice, presence, and sensing, and to communicate complex meaning through concise, established structures, proved to be a great way to develop leadership skills.

We have seen how savoir-relier makes sense in business. This final chapter will show how the principles of savoir-relier apply in other settings and make sense on a more general level as a tool for analysis, comprehension, and construction. We started with an analogy between leadership and horse riding; let's close by making the link between leadership and poetry.

POETIC VISION: THE BEAUTY OF STRUCTURE
AND FLEXIBILITY

Poetry brings a unique perspective to existing research in the field of complexity and relational leadership.[1] It demonstrates the sense that can emerge when we successfully manage tensions between opposing forces: freedom and control, creativity and rigor, vision and action, voice and power, sensibility and structure. What makes those contrasting elements work together is relationality. In poetry, relationality is best exemplified by metaphor (for example: "life is a journey") and metonymy (for example: "counting heads and noses" instead of "counting people"). These poetic devices establish relationships between different parts of the whole.[2] In this way, poetry becomes an example of a system. The combination of apparently contradicting forces facilitates a move from a siloed structure to a collaborative one where words in a poem—or individual minds in an organization—find their best expression through the shared sense that they build.

Many successful startups and creative organizations operate in this mode, combining rigor and creativity. One that is of particular interest because of its capacity to maintain its culture and identity within a larger organization is Pixar, the film animation studio that was bought by Disney in 2006. At Pixar, the power of relationships presents itself clearly in the words of Ed Catmull, co-founder of Pixar Animation Studios and president of Pixar and Disney Animation Studios: "Pixar is a community in the true sense of the word. We think that lasting relationships matter and we share some basic beliefs: talent is rare. Management's job is not to prevent risk but to build the capability to recover when failures occur. We must constantly challenge all of our assumptions and search for the flaws that could destroy our culture." He goes on, "The golden goal of development is not to find the good ideas; it is to put together the group of people that will function well together."[3]

Let us now see how we can draw lessons from poetry, from the way poems are composed, as a source of inspiration for both individual and organizational dimensions of leadership.

The Metaphor as a Leadership Device

A good metaphor implies an intuitive similarity between seemingly dissimilar elements: "life is a tree" or "love is a rose" are classic examples of metaphors.[4] As we saw previously in our discussion of Edgar Morin's early approach to complexity, order and disorder can be bound through interactions that find common ground between two opposites.[5] This line of thinking takes us from poetry into social science. Moving into business, metaphors have been employed in organizational theory for their capacity to generate knowledge, their "generative potential."[6]

Metaphors involve the transfer of information from a relatively familiar domain to one that is relatively unknown. Playing again with complexity, you can think of a metaphor as cross-domain mapping in a conceptual system.[7] Hence, metaphors permit a way of thinking of and seeing experiences. They are vehicles to address dynamic systems and create sense from the relationships that those systems foster. In practice, metaphors are a way to give people a sense of perspective, to take a step back from the situation they are in and see it from a different point of view.

A simple example of a metaphor in business can be found with corporate identity search. When a consulting or publicity firm is engaged by an organization that wishes to define or redefine its identity, many use metaphors to facilitate the search and delineate the image that will represent the values and vision of the company. Some test people's reactions to symbols and images in order to understand how the company perceives itself.

When the executive committee of HEC Paris decided to refresh its corporate identity following a major restructuring of its programs, we were presented with images like a unicorn, a boat, and a bridge to test and channel our perception of the school. Searching for a new logo and a new signature that would illustrate our image and drive our internationalization strategy to a new level, we brainstormed many options with the external agency that was leading the rebranding process. The words and images used in the creative process and the end result itself relied heavily on metaphorical and creative stages, in which individuals and groups of internal and external stakeholders expressed their opinions and ideas.

Every company from the smallest startup to the largest organization encounters the need to define its identity. This is a complex process where metaphors can serve as a great tool. In essence, they act as poetic devices. Building on metaphors facilitates critical moments of awareness that create a sense of purpose and can establish the direction that an organization may follow for years. Using these processes regularly is also a way to stay on your toes and challenge or revisit your strategic decisions in the light of new perspectives. Just as metaphors give a sense of perspective, poetry as whole can serve as a model to define the ingredients for leading in complexity.

Poetry Is Voice and Power

Poets draw on all the codes of language to produce a work of art, and in so doing they apprehend the world in its global dimension. The poet is this visionary, inspirational character incarnated by Walt Whitman in nineteenth-century America. Sometimes portrayed as a prophet for his capacity to inspire a whole generation with a message that continues to resonate, Whitman was the voice of democracy for America. He created enthusiasm in crowds of listeners through his voice, his words, and the expression of ideas that influenced the thoughts of an emerging country. His sounds and rhythms were bewildering to those who had a thirst for invention and new paths.[8] We find this in one of Whitman's poems from his collection *Leaves of Grass*:

"Voices," Walt Whitman

Now I make a leaf of Voices—for I have found nothing mightier than they are,
And I have found that no word spoken, but is beautiful, in its place.
O what is it in me that makes me tremble so at voices?
Surely, whoever speaks to me in the right voice, him or her I shall follow,
As the water follows the moon, silently, with fluid steps, anywhere around
　　the globe.
All waits for the right voices;
Where is the practis'd and perfect organ? Where is the develop'd Soul?
For I see every word utter'd thence, has deeper, sweeter, new sounds, impossible
　　on less terms.
I see brains and lips closed—tympans and temples unstruck,
Until that comes which has the quality to strike and to unclose,
Until that comes which has the quality to bring forth what lies slumbering,
　　forever ready, in all words.

Whitman praises the power of the voices, using a plural. The voices of the poets are associated with the voices of leadership, which contributes an early and interesting point of view on our relational leadership focus. This perspective of leadership in the plural contradicts the approach of the leader as a single individual who holds the vision and values for all followers. Whitman challenges the image of the charismatic leader with an idea of leadership that stems from interactions between people, voices, and viewpoints. Whitman's poem further speaks of "the right voices," the ones to be followed with no limits. This poem could very well be titled "The Voices of Leadership": voices that have "the quality to strike and to unclose, . . . the quality to bring forth what lies slumbering, forever ready, in all words."

Voice is the expression of the mind with its personal touch or sensibility. It is what all leaders are looking for: a genuine capacity to express from within the values and message that will drive their listeners in the same direction. The voice is tone, music, and sense. In poetry, voices are free and coded, sensible and structured. The paradox of poetry is the same paradox that modern organizations face: to reconcile the creativity necessary to build new environments and remain competitive with the rigor that is indispensable if that creativity is to be channeled in a sensible direction. Understanding the poetic paradox then becomes a way to address our leadership paradox.

Poetry Is Action and Vision

The primary sense of poetry comes from the Latin word *poein*, which means "to make." Poetry is action and creation; poetry crafts words that depict the world as it is, in its natural complexity. Poetry uses language not only to express ideas and visions, but also to generate images, sounds, and emotions. Poetry is language in its utmost complexity; to use a metaphor, poetry is complexity. Words weave together to create a message. They make sense by drawing on the associations or relationships created between words, as well as the sounds and images thrown up by those words. Poetic language is mind in action.[9] Action is revealed by the poem that presents a sensible view of a situation and builds a relationship between the mind of the poet and the reader.

The French surrealist poet Paul Eluard spoke of a poem as a combined multitude of terms submitted to the necessities of reality that weave in time and space to create continuous action and stable atmosphere.[10] More plainly stated, poetic rhythm, syntax, imagery, and phonemic organization coexist to build the system that we call a poem. Action—these elements working within the system of the poem—is a powerful element that is inherent to poetry. Leadership suffers when action is not directly connected to vision, as it is in the case of poetry.

Eluard speaks of the vast spreads of night that poetry dissolves and says that poetry is the art of lights. These lights lead our vision and enable us to make sense of poems with an apparently simple set of tools: words. The light metaphor is particularly relevant for companies that lose their way or part of their identity when they face a merger, an acquisition, or simply a core change.

Here is a poem by Robert Frost, "Fire and Ice," that will illustrate a vision stemming from his act of writing. With this poem, I will engage you in a three-step exercise to help you develop your savoir-relier leadership skill set. You should read the poem once silently in your head, then pause and write down your first impressions in a few lines to gather your initial holistic impressions of the vision the poem is communicating.

"Fire and Ice," Robert Frost
Some say the world will end in fire,
Some say in ice.
From what I've tasted of desire
I hold with those who favor fire.
But if it had to perish twice,
I think I know enough of hate
To say that for destruction ice
Is also great
And would suffice.

This is the vision: the end of relationships is the end of the world. The poet's experience and perception is that passion can lead to destruction, whether that occurs through the heat of anger or the coldness of hatred.

As a leader, how can you communicate your vision as powerfully as Frost does? As we saw with Walt Whitman, the first tool that poets use for effective communication is their voice.

Moving on with our exercise, I suggest you explore Frost's vision with a second reading of "Fire and Ice," this time out loud to yourself or to an audience. Once you have done this, answer the following questions in writing: Can you hear the iambic rhythm with its repetitive combination of unstressed and stressed syllables? "Some say the world will end in fire": Do you see the rhymes that connect the words together? What is the effect of your voice when you read the poem aloud compared to when you read it silently? How does your voice interact with the poet's voice? By answering these questions, you are moving from a holistic and intuitive perception of the poem to a more analytical stage that unfolds the structure and processes that make the vision exist. The poem is a text, an interface between the poet and you, the reader, just as an organization is an interface between the people who work for it and its stakeholders.

In "Fire and Ice," Frost presents us with two possibilities for the world's destruction in reference to a common scientific debate of his time: some scientists argued that a new ice age would destroy all living things on the planet, while others said that the world would be incinerated from its volcanic core. But Frost chose to give a personal and emotional side to the debate, associating desire with fire and hatred with ice. This metaphorical view of the two elements makes the "world" in this poem a metaphor for relationships. Despite the initial dichotomy between fire and ice in the first two lines of the poem and the leaning toward fire induced by the narrator, the poem acknowledges that both elements could destroy the world. Frost also introduces his personal experience with desire and hatred to show that fire and ice are not mutually exclusive. In fact, he ultimately admits that fire and ice are quite similar in terms of their power to destroy.

Power is a critical element in leadership contexts. Power and influence are commonly attributed to leaders who can inspire people. But we rarely talk about how power is exercised because the exercise of power is so controversial: it can be the source of both good and bad leadership, even when the principles applied are fairly similar. With the example of poetry, I suggest that three key factors subtend positive power mechanisms:

a combination of action and vision, a careful use of voice and its capacity to express power, and a delicate association of sensibility and structure.

Poetry Binds Structure and Sensibility

Poetry is highly structured and based on codes, metrics, systems, and symbols. These create rhythms and music that carry messages, paint visions, and blend imagination and thought. From its original oral tradition, poetry has evolved over time into very controlled forms. Poets experiment with these forms, building new graphics and forms to make the structure evolve to fit new movements and ways of thinking.

Composing a sonnet, an ode, or a sestina requires respect for very specific rules covering rhyme patterns and rhythms. For example, the iambic pentameter is used in English, while the Alexandrine is the rule in French poetry. Each language has its codes that poetry makes universal through poetic figures such as alliteration, simile, and metaphor. These processes and devices channel the poet's vision. They facilitate the transmission of the poet's visions and values. They belong to the coding system of poetic language that structures meaning into forms and builds sense for the reader, just as leaders use processes to share values among people in the organization.

What is interesting about structure is that each poet builds on traditional codes of meter, rhyme, and rhythm to create his or her own living ecosystem where each poem has a place and plays a role in expressing the vision of the poet. A poem embodies both form and meaning. "Form is the vessel in which the meaning is cast. They need each other reciprocally as in an association of soul and body."[11] Poets have reinvented traditional forms over time, like the sonnet, which has evolved from the Petrarchan to the Elizabethan or Shakespearean and now has a modern form, which is different again. Poets write and revise their poems hundreds of times, reaching for the form that matches the vision they wish to communicate.

A poem is an organization in which words are people and poetic structure is the system that drives sense. The poet is the entrepreneur who builds the system and makes it work in its complexity. The process takes time and ongoing effort. The poet has to experiment and make constant revisions as he or she works to overcome errors and failures and make progress. This dimension of writing—the need for revision and reinvention—reflects the work of a leader who needs to keep questioning and trying and making mistakes in order to find new avenues, new solutions. We will now see how the structure of a poem drives the vision and sense by relying on codes and devices.

Frost's poem is written in iambic rhythm and has lines of eight or four syllables. The words correspond: it is because the word *desire* is at the end of verse three and rhymes with *fire* that we associate the two words; the crossed rhymes of *twice, ice,* and *suffice* bring together Frost's powerful message about the fear of a world ending by fire or by ice. These links strengthen the meaning and give sense to the relationships built therein. Another device used in poetry that can apply to leadership is repetition. In *Leaves of Grass*, Whitman often uses repetition or anaphora as a poetic device to stress his ideas. Repetition is, indeed, a powerful teaching and speech device that can be useful when delivering difficult or complex messages to team members, colleagues, or crowds. Many other poetic devices are deployed by political speechwriters. Bill Clinton's inauguration speech of 1993, for example, was filled with rhymes and alliterations.

To better understand structure, let us go back to our exercise and approach Frost's poem for a third reading, silent again. When you are done, write out the answers to the following questions. What does the poem inspire in you? How does it make you feel? What do you see and imagine after reading it for the third time? Do you like the poem? If so, why? And if not, why not?

This three-step exercise is a method to understand complex issues, situations, or problems. You move from your initial, intuitive, and sensible impression to an analytical approach and, finally, make sense of the poem for yourself through emotional and mindful understanding. By confronting your first impression with the structure and analysis of the subject in the poem (the destruction of the world), then following that with an assessment of the feelings and sensations you perceive (relationships led by fire/desire or ice/coldness), you rebuild the sense of the poem in a complex unity that carries both literal meaning (the scientific debate about the end of the world) and figurative meaning (how relationships can be destroyed as easily by too much passion as by hatred).

When Structure Meets Sensibility in Business

Let's pause here to consider how structure and sensibility combine in an organization. L'Oréal is a French cosmetics company that operates globally. The leader of their Division of Professional Products (DPP), which produces the world's leading professional hair-color brand, was concerned about getting the chemical engineers who develop the products to understand the needs of the hairdressers who use them. The idea was that the best way to get a product that suited the end customer was to tap into the hairdressers' desire to provide a perfect hair color.

It was decided that engaging the hairdressers in the product development process as partners, rather than as consumers, would resolve the tension. The product development team fostered innovation by making beauty the driver for everyone involved in the process. The aesthetic dimension facilitated the work of the technicians and engineers in their labs, and it also facilitated the creative promotional work undertaken by the marketing teams. The process entailed regular exchanges in open-space settings where both engineers and hairdressers would meet to test and discuss the end use of the developed product. Usually, those two key players in the innovation process would be kept separate.

This association between the engineers and the hairdressers is comparable to the words in the poem—with L'Oréal serving as the system in which interaction takes place, like a poem itself. The unique combination of engineers and hairdressers and the structure that binds them—this shared project—created meaning in the form of a better product and served a vision, that of beauty.

By creating common ground motivated by aesthetics, the sensibility shown by the L'Oréal DPP team created a place for expression right alongside technical and rational sources of knowledge. Yet sensibility is scary because it shows human fragility and vulnerability. Ultimately, this vulnerability and fragility is a source of strength because it conveys a critical element of good leadership: humility—the strength to recognize that we are not perfect, that we are not machines, that we are human, that we are fragile and breakable. Being fragile and vulnerable, being aware of one's fragility, is the first step toward self-awareness and a source of strength.

In poetry, the structure does not constrain the message and the words. On the contrary, it sets them free to combine and build new meaning. Writing poetry is a process, a continuous movement that weaves between the need for structure and the right to freedom that poets exercise through their creations. This is precisely what organizations need to look for: devices, processes, and structures that serve to structure, but not to restrain, the range of responses necessary to face a rapidly changing world. Thinking about what makes poetry powerful and how those elements of power can be harnessed in leadership is but one angle for us to examine. From our understanding of poetry, let us now delineate the principles of relationality and their relevance to leadership.

Poetry and the Principles of Relationality

Through their writing, poets inspire and engage people in their generation and for generations to come. This is why I encourage those of you who seek better leadership to use writing as a means of consciousness and awareness. The poet's vision lies in the union between what is perceived and what is thought or imagined, between reality and dreams. Relationality is the mechanism that poets use to influence readers. Expressed another way, the poet rebuilds language to imbue it with complex meaning by capitalizing on its relational power. I argue that we need to include all three sources of knowledge—rational, sensible, and emotional—to better apprehend our surroundings and make sense of the world as the poets do.

Indeed, to grasp the essence of a poem, one must feel it, sense it, and deeply understand the whole and each part of the whole. The relationships that are created in this process are sources of sense building that make the whole poem flow. The whole is the message, the "big picture," the vision carried by the poem. We see this with "Fire and Ice" and in its relationships to the other poems that Robert Frost wrote. A poem is a living ecosystem, which operates in a larger ecosystem—the poet's complete works—just as a division, branch, or function operates in the larger ecosystem of an organization.

The analogies between poems and organizations are multiple. Words can be seen as people, project teams, units, divisions, or functions in the organization. How each entity relates to the others is the crux of leadership, just as the power of a poem stems from the relationships built between the words within it and with the rest of the poet's work. The poem is also a point of connection with an outside world of readers and listeners, equivalent to the stakeholders for organizations. It is in these relationships that sense making and sense building are to be found. It is in the way that people, teams, functions, and units interact with or respond to one another and with external stakeholders that an organization builds its own course of action. By building a living ecosystem that understands the rules and codes in which it moves, the leaders in the organization lay the groundwork for effective and fruitful associations in which each person or function has a clear position relative to the other.

This is another lesson to be learned from the poets: the power of relationality creates fluidity and flexibility in roles and relationships according to four now-familiar principles: perception, reliance, resilience, and responsibility.

Principle 1: Perception.   Before the mental act of writing can commence, the poet must perceive. Relationality begins with the perception of the environment. The poet Charles Baudelaire expresses this beautifully in his poem "Correspondences," saying "perfumes, colors, tones answer each other" and "there are perfumes fresh as children's flesh."[12]

Perception relies on a particular use of the senses that is at the origin of a different kind of relationship. The reader of poetry is moved by the power of words to see images, strike beats, and hear sounds that are the reflections of the poet's soul, emotions, and sensibility. Perception precedes emotion; it is a necessary step to connect to the world of sensible data and creates the conditions for reliance to occur.

Principle 2: Reliance.   For the relationship to thrive, a second principle applies: reliance. In poetry, the act of writing finds its force in the act of reading. There is no hierarchical power of the poet over the reader. Instead, there is an interplay between the poet, who builds sense via the medium of the poem, and the reader, who builds sense from his or her perception of, feelings about, and understanding of the poem. This relationship is reciprocal and requires a strong reliance on the other. To pursue this exchange with respect depends on confidence in one's self and trust in the other.

Principle 3: Resilience.   More often than not, poets relate to the dark and troubled sides of relationships and show resilience by expressing their hardship through their vision and perception of their environment. The poet-reader relationship is a source of knowledge creation. The poet's intention is often to bring to the surface the reader's own resilience by stimulating her mind, senses, and emotions.

Moreover, writing itself becomes an act of resilience because the poet must reminisce and bring to light difficult thoughts, experiences, and relationships. In the same way, the reader builds resilience by confronting personal experience through reading. This is an example of what Chris Argyris calls "double loop learning," namely the capacity to alter a goal or even reject it in the light of experience when repeated efforts to achieve it are unsuccessful. This inspires our work on resilience as a powerful leadership skill.

Principle 4: Responsibility.   Both poet and reader have a responsibility in their relationship: to generate sense from their encounter. The poet has a certain sense in mind while writing the poem, but the reader also has a responsibility to receive, interpret, and make sense of the poem from his or her own perspective. This shared responsibility can be compared to that of the leader-follower relationship with a new twist: it is mutual and shared as opposed to top-down.

Transposed into the realm of the organization, particularly with the evolution toward flatter companies, this poet-reader interplay highlights the possibility for greater flexibility or agility of roles. The relationship then functions like a partnership in which different people may step up at different times.

This aspect of leadership is clearly visible in the example of co-creation at Alcatel-Lucent, where project teams or "scrum teams" delineate roles that are dynamic and may change as the project emphasis changes from product creation to customer use. The customer is also engaged in the design. No one is stuck in a given role; people can lead the group one day and observe or follow the next day. But to accept this fluid interplay, individuals must demonstrate perceptiveness, reliance, resilience, and responsibility. They must have enough respect and humility to step down from a leadership role and support their colleague's leadership when that is what best serves the team's objective. Fluidity combined with flexibility defines the relational leadership stance. It entails shared responsibility rather than a leadership team in which responsibility is owned by a single authority figure.

This does not mean, however, that there is no leader. Instead it means that the leader's role is fluid because roles and responsibilities vary in time and space. Leaders always have bosses and stakeholders, so their role depends on their position and the relationships involved at a given moment. Understanding and facilitating flexibility and fluidity is a critical factor of effective leadership today. The challenge with this approach is a form of instability induced by too much flexibility or agility. Movement and balance are senses that help grow the capacity for change. But most people resist change and prefer stability and stillness, which are safer and more reassuring. The risk of a leadership technique that encourages agility and role fluidity lies in the fact that power is challenged when different people influence its structure.

Leaders in need of authority are particularly fearful of letting go and feel challenged by the risk of losing power and control when new players can take the lead. These questions also relate to positional and personal leadership, which engage both individual and social dimensions to establish new kinds of interplay in traditionally exclusive lines of research and practice. To further explore these ideas for better leadership, I will now move from poetry to poetic translation, from the poem as a source text for a first reader to the poem as a target text for a new reader in a different language. Poetic translation is a perfect illustration of the savoir-relier process.

POETIC TRANSLATION: RE-CREATING SENSE
IN TIMES OF CHANGE

The first poem that I translated was *New Fires*, a neo-epic poem written by my then English professor and friend, Larry D. Griffin. It is a long poem filled with images of Texas and Oklahoma where the poet lived, the reflections of a man inspired by the voice of Walt Whitman. I was fortunate to share his vision and perception because I lived in the same places and spent time with him. I could see what he saw and feel how he felt.

This understanding—my ability to comprehend the thoughts, feelings, emotions, and perceptions of the poet before reading his words—was an incredible discovery in the voyage of translation. I felt pure empathy. I was able to step inside the mind and dreams of the author before translating this poem into French, my native language, to give a new birth to the poem in a new context for new readers.

The act of translation uncovered two primary skills that I later found critical in leadership: self-awareness and empathy. The second translation I tackled was *Nadja*, a novel by the French surrealist André Breton. This second cross-cultural voyage began with the first words of the book: "Who am I?" Indeed, translating *Nadja* was a way for me to look inside my own culture and language, to look inside myself. It became a highly introspective process: feeling at home in the French language became a way for me to cope with being far away from my French homeland.

Enjoying the work of translation, both for its capacity to foster new reader-author relationships across continents and for the access it provides to different viewpoints, led me to develop a personal approach to poetic translation. My approach reflects this dynamic, systemic relationship between the languages, texts, or poems.

My journey in the literal act of translation highlights the importance of self-awareness and voice in being a translator of complex texts between different languages. Developing those qualities is necessary to build the confidence to engage in the act of translation itself, an act comparable to the act of leadership, as we shall now see.

Translation and Management: Different Roles at Different Levels

Translation, like leadership, involves "moving in a certain direction." Some argue that translating poetry is impossible; Robert Frost says, "Poetry is what gets lost in translation." The linguist Roman Jakobson contends that translating poetry is impossible yet imperative and that only a creative transposition is possible.[13] However, as we observe with Umberto Eco, translation has always existed.[14] We only have to look at the example of holy texts, which have been read by millions of people in a multitude of languages over the centuries. Stories have always been passed from one person to another, written down, and rewritten. Translation is an integral component of our need to share and disseminate knowledge, our basic human need to move forward. *Traduction*, the French word for "translation," comes directly from the Latin *traducere*, where *tra* or *tran* refers to the notion of movement and *ducere* to the notion of direction, that is, to move toward a certain direction.[15]

This basic need for movement complies with the notion of relational leadership and complex dynamic systems, which require movement or the transfer of knowledge and action to lead the way. The role of translation is to facilitate movement and to indicate the direction of sense. With poetics, I define translation as a process that moves a text from one language system, the source language, to another language system, the target language, through an act of re-creation that respects the relationships and completeness of the original.[16] It is vital to bear in mind that the translator has to make choices. He or she has to decide what to leave aside and what to retain or rebuild in the work to make the move in the right direction. Leaders too have to decide where to cut costs, where to invest in order to maintain their organization's growth, and how to move forward in times of crises.

Interestingly, there are differences between translating a technical document and a literary or poetic one that can map differences in translation skills based on different roles within organizations. I have identified four levels of translation as illustrated in Figure 7.1, which can be associated with four major roles in business: technical, managerial, entrepreneurial, and sense-relational. Let's explore each of these roles.

Technical Expertise.   The first level of translation requires expertise in the source language and in the target language. Knowing the right words, grammar, and syntax are essential skills for anyone seeking to translate a technical document, such as the maintenance manual for an airplane. The text must be extremely precise. It must describe the parts of the plane and the actions to be taken so that the technicians engage in the correct actions. Any mistake in the translation of the manual could have terrible consequences.

The execution of such translations requires scientific precision. The translation must be exact and undertaken with the sole goal of rendering

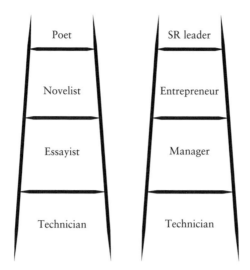

FIGURE 7.1   Four levels of translation and organizational roles

the original instructions of the author as exactly as possible to ensure that all readers receive the same information. Already, this example is likely to have you thinking of the experts and technicians within organizations. Experts bring the knowledge and skills that are the fuel of innovation and development.

Managerial Competence. The second level involves a different set of skills because human interpretation and context begin to play a role. In an essay, the intention of the author has a meaning that goes beyond the simple sharing of knowledge or information. The focus is on informing the reader of real facts and bringing information, observation, raw data, and rational thinking to light. This role requires an understanding of the writer's culture and environment so as to communicate, effectively and directly, the ideas presented or the facts observed. The main objective is to transfer information with accuracy.

Similarly, the translator of essays must have a good command of the subject explored by the essayist in order to translate the reasoning and the sequencing of the text. There is little room for freedom and intuition. This level of translation occurs more often in rational environments than in intuitive ones. Nevertheless, the relational and contextual dimensions are still important. This role corresponds to that of the manager in an organization who is responsible for coordinating work and contextualizing projects. The emphasis is on performance and structure. The manager needs to have the relational and coordination skills to create conditions, processes, and working environment that project teams need to thrive.

Entrepreneurial Vision. The third level appeals to a more complex set of skills and draws on more imaginative and creative areas of the mind. The translator of a novel requires a capacity to analyze and understand the intention of the author. In business, this means being able to work with people's intentions and desires through a deep understanding of individual motivations and aspirations. Translating fiction requires the capacity to build on the symbolic nature of the text and its references to the imagination of the author. In business, this implies a capacity to make decisions based on an understanding of the sense and relationships that drive the organization. This is a much more complex task; rational thinking does not suffice. This role is that of a traditional leader in a postmodern organization who creates an entrepreneurial environment around his or her vision in order to drive the company and its people forward.

The Poetic Translator in Command of Savoir-Relier

With the fourth level, the act of translation addresses language as a complex mix of interconnections between images, sounds, rhythms, symbols, and words. The final act is that of reenunciation or re-creation, the function of which is to maintain the rhythmic unity of the original and present it to a new reader in another language. If a part is lost, the whole is lost. If meaning and images are kept but the sounds, rhythms, and associations are left aside, little of the original poem will remain. I argue that poetic translation cannot take place unless the translator is herself a poet.

Keeping complex, dynamic unity in translation to rebuild sense is the very function of savoir-relier. The relational capacity of a leader is best exemplified by the poetic translator's role and the process used. The act of poetic translation is comparable to the act of leadership through the strategic decision-making processes it entails as well as their execution.

The process that subtends effective poetic translation leads the way to the mechanisms that make relationality and sense building work together.

Translation here involves a process of re-creation that rebuilds sense out of complex, ambiguous, and heterogeneous associations. It is different from the process developed to translate a technical or literary document. This role highlights new skills distinct from those of the traditional leader and emphasizes the complexity of the context in which these leaders operate. These are leaders in a new paradigm; these are savoir-relier leaders. With poetic translation as a model, we will now see the paradigm in which these pioneers operate.

Translating the Complex: A Living Ecosystem Emerging from Relationality

Figure 7.2 illustrates the analogy between poetic translation theory and the world of organizations, seen as living ecosystems. The common denominator between the two environments is relationality. Let's analyze how the ecosystem functions.

The heart of the company is composed of the human beings that work for it. Each individual joins the company with a particular personality, motivation, drive, and set of skills that are relevant to their position and enable them to play their role. As soon as they enter the company,

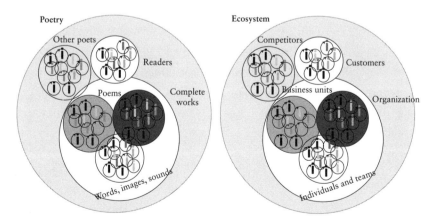

FIGURE 7.2 From poetry to the living ecosystem

relationality begins, just as the poet enters a relationship when the reader discovers his or her poems. In the company, the first level of relationality is between two individuals who interact with each other. Such relationships can be worker-worker, worker-customer, or worker-manager, to name but three. With relational coordination and recent research in relational bureaucracy,[17] a hybrid form of organization has emerged combining the network form and the bureaucratic form. It associates the value of relationships with traditional hierarchical models.

We need to define the mind-set that subtends interactions between two individuals at all levels in this living ecosystem. In common with relational coordination and the relational bureaucracy hybrid form, the savoir-relier mind-set defines relationships through the notions of care, reciprocity, shared goals, shared knowledge, and mutual respect. Southwest Airlines, for example, is a company that has grown to become one of the largest airlines in the world while emphasizing the importance of respect and reciprocal relationships in the workplace. To quote one Southwest pilot: "You see that guy coming up from the ramp to tell me about the weight and balance on this plane? I don't even know him and I respect him. And I know he respects me."[18] We find a similar message when a gate agent speaks of the worker-customer relationship: "The customer is not always right. We treat the customer like family, like we do with everyone else, but that doesn't mean they are always right. They can't be abusive to us or to other customers."[19]

The implications for leadership are numerous because the living ecosystem we define here cannot operate effectively without a fusion between the individual sense and the collective sense. Once these principles are in place and become core operating values of the company, the same mind-set applies to team interactions. Again, we turn to Southwest Airlines and the relationship that has developed there between workers and managers: "We work very hard so that anyone can walk in here with a problem. We'll work on it together and figure out how to do it better next time. Maybe you screwed up. When you leave, you have self-esteem." An organization that values interpersonal and reciprocal respect will develop a leadership that binds order, structure, and individual freedom and initiatives. To achieve such balance requires intensive work on the ecosystem's dynamics.

From individuals and teams, we move to more complex cells of the ecosystem with units, branches, divisions, or functions. Everyone knows and has faced the tensions between the R&D or engineering department and the marketing department, or between different regions, which develop and sell different products or brands under the same overarching organization. The "us versus them" syndrome is commonly expressed as soon as a subculture develops within a group that has a specific task to complete or has built its own living system within the larger ecosystem.

Pernod Ricard, for example, has a large array of brands such as Chivas, Ballantine's, Absolut, and Mumm's Champagne. Conviviality is part of their identity, and each individual and group working with Pernod Ricard, whether they are in China or Greece, working with Chivas or Absolut, is expected to adopt a convivial mind-set. The company develops strategies to spread the meaning and usage of conviviality or "the art of living together," which implies sharing, caring, and respect, while bearing in mind that conviviality may manifest itself differently in different cultures. The ecosystem works effectively when all the constitutive elements of the system, including relationships with customers and competitors, move in line with this sense of conviviality. The challenge is to maintain this dynamic at all levels of the organization to prevent different interpretations and splits between different units emerging.

Our next step is to look at ways to develop a strategy that fosters a balanced ecosystem capable of adapting in real time to the changes induced by a global and uncertain business environment. To do so, let us go back to our poetic translation model. We will look more closely at the different roles the translator-poet plays as he or she makes the transformation from the original poem and its original readers to the translated poem and its new readers. These roles are comparable to those played by savoir-relier leaders as they apply relationality principles within the relational circuit.

Savoir-Relier: A Leadership Process Inspired by Poetic Translation
We can draw further lessons from poetic translation by looking at the different roles the poet-translator takes on at different stages of the process:

1. The holistic reader grasps the overall meaning and complex nature of the text through intuitive and sensible perception.

2. The analytical reader analyzes, decomposes, and decodes not only the meaning of the words but also their complex relationships, interconnections, connotations, and symbolic references as experienced by the author, as well as the rhyme schemes, rhythms, and images they produce.

3. The relational reader assimilates the multiple dimensions of the text by looking at how the parts connect and relate within a complex unity in the ecosystem of poetry.

4. The relational writer engages in "decentering."[20]

5. The sense writer re-creates the essence and sense of the original text. This act encompasses subjective self-knowledge, as well as knowledge and experience of the other author and language with its codes, references, and culture, in order to form a new text. This re-creation involves decision making and risk-taking in the selection of words, syntax, and images and in the use of symbols, images, sounds, and rhythms. It is a process that rebuilds the relationships from the original text into the new, target-language system where the new poem will take form.

The final moment, the outcome, occurs when a new reader in the target language discovers the text and understands it; when he or she sees, hears, and feels ideas, sensations, and emotions that are comparable to those experienced by readers of the original work. The role of the translator can be compared to that of a mediator between two experiences in different complex language systems, each of whom has their own references and codes drawn from their own history and culture, each existing in a different time and space. The translator-poet goes further, however, and becomes the "rewriter" who re-creates the ambiguous and complex associations of the original by defining new associations in a different language. As we have seen, similar roles apply to business settings with the relational circuit.

In the end, poetry is a unique place to understand the complex associations that subtend our day-to-day problems. To illustrate this point, I chose an extract from Elizabeth Bishop's poem, "At the Fishhouses," where she uses the metaphor of the sea to discuss knowledge:

"At the Fishhouses," Elizabeth Bishop
I have seen it over and over, the same sea, the same,
slightly, indifferently swinging above the stones,
icily free above the stones,
above the stones and then the world. [. . .]
It is like what we imagine knowledge to be:
Dark, salt, clear, moving, utterly free,
Drawn from the cold hard mouth
of the world, derived from the rocky breasts
forever, flowing and drawn, and since
our knowledge is historical, flowing, and flown.

The water image tells us that our knowledge is founded on the multiplicity of sources it indefinitely flows from and into. As savoir-relier leaders, we must base our knowledge on the association of disjointed sources, such as the biological and cultural, the psychological and sociological, the subjective and historical, the individual and collective, the personal and interpersonal, the organizational and institutional. Our knowledge must also reconcile contradictions and serve divergent purposes to flow and build sense for others.

To be effective, the integration of all these subjects or sources of knowledge requires a capacity for self-effacement and humility in order to make room for new observations outside our typical view. The sense of complexity arising from our incapacity to be certain about everything or to avoid contradictions forces humility and lends to a sense of solidarity. Everything is interdependent and proves the multidimensional character of reality.

Our inner complexity makes of each of us an individual cosmos. This is where we must begin if we are to apprehend reality and act as leaders. At the level of the leader, the two dimensions, *savoir* and *relier*, are based on the complementary and balanced binding of rationality and sensibility, of objectivity and subjectivity. However, few leaders dare to claim that intuition or "gut feeling" is critical in their decision-making process.

I have argued that by integrating subjectivity into their observation and analysis, leaders open the door to reliable sensibility. Leaders can translate their experience, their understanding of the environment, their confidence, their sensible intelligence, and their courage into meaningful and mindful action. In this way, we redefine leadership by its relational and sensible dimensions to engage in positive and mindful innovation, the central consequence of savoir-relier as applied to organizational theory. The process of organizational innovation is multidimensional: it has elements of individual psychology in the personal and cognitive dimensions, but also the group and organizational dimensions. The implication is that fostering creativity and innovation in organizations cannot simply be confined to giving individuals "creativity tools." The process needs to be systemic and *trans*disciplinary if it is to include the inquirer in the inquiry, the innovator in the innovation.

Our journey of discovery has taken us from mundane water-cooler conversations to "Eureka!" moments at Chinese street-food stalls, from ailing multinationals that have lost their way to thriving family companies with an eye on the future, from uninspired managers imposing cookie-cutter methodologies to a new generation of thoughtful individuals who are creating success by building sense. Inspired by poetic translation, we have engaged in avenues where leadership means more than self-serving profit and found the value of being an individual or an organization with genuine, generous, and generative mind-sets that operate with sense.

Why does sense matter? It matters because it enables us to embrace complexity and navigate a complicated world in constant motion. It enables leaders to build strong relationships, make confident decisions, and identify overarching goals that provide stability in times of change. It underpins the triangular relationship between structure, freedom, and relationality that is a necessary condition for managing the tensions that are inherent in business and in everyday life. Sense is the common thread that lets a jazz ensemble perform a familiar tune with flair and panache at the same moment that they are reinventing it through on-the-spot improvisation.

Sense matters because our senses matter. Opening our ears and our eyes and paying attention to the messages in our environment is a path to greater insight and understanding. Awareness, attention, observation, empathy, and curiosity enhance our capacity to innovate and ability to build relationships. Our senses help us leverage the world around us and the ties that bind us to solve problems and make decisions.

The journey to successful leadership depends on creating sense out of our environment and communicating that to everyone involved. I wish to share the real story of an airline captain, one of very few women in the world qualified to fly Boeing 777 aircraft, as a parting example. She and her husband decided to reach out to people who are rejected by society. In April 2010, she bought an abandoned orphanage in Sologne, France; in less than two years, with the help of former convicts and drug addicts, she had transformed it into a thirty-bedroom conference venue. Although she drew on her leadership experience as captain, it was her desire to build sense that gave her the courage to start. The desire to change something in society, to act with the genuine and generous mind-set, gave her strength and power to address difficult tensions. When most who see the homeless or people rejected by society do nothing, our airline captain decided she would give her energy and time to build a structure where those people would have a place and a role to play.

She and her husband trusted their instincts and worked hard to build the unlikely and complex relationships that were necessary to take an idea about occupational and social integration and bring it to fruition in the form of a successful business. They opened their door to former convicts, drug addicts, and homeless people who felt they had no future and gave them a new chance in life with the perspective of building something new that would make sense. By guiding them into renovating this old orphanage, together they gave life to a place that would become a welcoming and efficient location to host business seminars. They realized that they could build sense relationships for themselves and the world. You can do the same, now, within your organization or outside.

The poet opens his or her mind to the world as it is. He or she experiences it, considers it, reinvents it, and returns it to us in a form that enables us to make new sense of our emotions and our surroundings. A poet's success depends on the intensity of her attention, on her ability to forge new connections between disparate ideas, and on her capacity to express those connections in a way that speaks to her audience. That audience must be open to experiences, aware of their surroundings, confident in their instincts, thoughtful in their conclusions, and bold enough to risk rejection when sharing new ideas.

The translator finds a path between what is expressed and what is understood. His inquiring, analytical mind enables him to unpack what is essential in the poet's experience; his sensitivity and open spirit enable him to generate new concepts that express a renewed understanding of the poet's experience. He is creative within established boundaries, innovative while respecting parameters, and able to transform the existent into something new.

The leader—the savoir-relier leader—is a poet and translator: he or she builds sense and creates positive relationships through attention to the world and the people who surround him or her; such leaders are open to new ideas and able to connect them in innovative ways; they inspire confidence because they understand the value of humility, resilience, and honesty. Adopt the poet-translator's approach to life: train yourself to observe your environment and the people who surround you; focus your energy on understanding, imagining, and empathizing; and have the courage to express your ideas and challenge preconceptions. Above all, be genuine, generous, and generative.

NOTES

CHAPTER 1

1. Intuition is an important constituent of savoir-relier, but this is not the place for an in-depth debate on the role of intuition in business. For literature about intuition in business and psychology, I recommend the following works, among many others: W. H. Agor (ed.), *Intuition in Organizations: Leading and Managing Productively* (Newbury Park, CA: Sage, 1989); M. Crossan, H. Lane, and R. White, "An Organizational Learning Framework: From Intuition to Institution," *Academy of Management Review* 24, no. 3 (1999); G. Klein, *Intuition at Work* (New York: Random House, 2003); E. Sadler-Smith, *Inside Intuition* (New York: Routledge, 2008); and J. Parikh, *Intuition: The New Frontier of Management* (Oxford, UK: Blackwell, 1994).

2. R. E. Miles, G. Miles, C. C. Snow, K. Blomqvist, and H. Rocha, "The I-Form Organization," *California Management Review* 51, no. 4 (2009): 61–76.

3. J. Reingold and R. Underwood, "Was 'Built to Last' Built to Last?" November 1, 2004, http://www.fastcompany.com/50992/was-built-last-built-last.

4. N. N. Taleb, *The Black Swan* (New York: Random House, 2010); N. N. Taleb, *The Black Swan: The Impact of the Highly Improbable* (London: Penguin, 2007).

5. Taleb, *The Black Swan*, 169.

6. R. Girard, *Deceit, Desire, and the Novel: Self and Other in Literary Structure*, trans. Y. Frecerro (Baltimore: Johns Hopkins University Press, 1965). Originally published in French as *Mensonge romantique, vérité romanesque* (Paris: Grasset, 1961; new edition by Hachette Pluriel in 2009).

7. For an overview of charismatic, transactional, transformational, and situational leadership, see the following reference books: J. A. Conger and R. N. Kanungo (eds.), *Charismatic Leadership in Organizations* (Thousand Oaks, CA: Sage, 1998); P. Hersey and K. Blanchard, *Management of Organizational Behavior: Utilizing Human Resources*, 3rd ed. (Englewood Cliffs, NJ: Prentice Hall, 1977); J. M. Burns, *Leadership* (New York: Harper & Row, 1978); J. M. Burns, *Transforming Leadership: A New Pursuit of Happiness* (New York: Atlantic Monthly Press, 2003); B. M. Bass, *Leadership and Performance beyond Expectations* (New York: Free Press, 1985); B. M. Bass and R. E. Riggio, *Transformational Leadership*, 2nd ed. (Mahwah, NJ: Erlbaum, 2006); and S. J. Musser, *The Determination of Positive and Negative Charismatic Leadership* (Grantham, PA: Messiah College, 1987).

8. Aristotle, *de Mundo* 5b12, p. 396, quoted in Athenaeum Library of Philosophy, http://evans-experientialism.freewebspace.com/heraclitus01.htm.

9. B. Pascal, *Pensées* [Thoughts], trans. T. S. Eliot (New York: Dutton, 1958), 20. Originally published in 1669.

10. E. Morin, "Beyond Determinism: The Dialogue of Order and Disorder," *SubStance* 40 (1983): 22–35; E. Morin, *La complexité humaine* [Human complexity] (Paris: Flammarion, 1994); E. Morin, *On Complexity* (Cresskill, NJ: Hampton Press, 2008).

11. Morin, *On Complexity*, 49.

12. Ibid., 62.

13. K. Weick, "Sense and Reliability," *Harvard Business Review* (May 2009): 84–90.

CHAPTER 2

1. Personal interview with Clara Gaymard, October 19, 2012.

2. Ibid.

3. Ibid.

4. Ibid.

5. W. Bennis and J. O'Toole, "The Culture of Candor," *Harvard Business Review* (June 2009); W. Bennis, D. Goleman, and J. O'Toole, *Transparency: How Leaders Create a Culture of Candor* (San Francisco: Jossey-Bass, 2008).

6. S. Culbert, *Beyond Bullsh*t: Straight-Talk at Work* (Stanford, CA: Stanford University Press, 2008).

7. Bennis and O'Toole, "The Culture of Candor," 3.

8. B. George and P. Sims, *True North: Discover Your Authentic Leadership* (San Francisco: Jossey-Bass, 2007).

9. A. G. Lafley, "'I Think of My Failures as a Gift,'" *Harvard Business Review* (April 2011), 86–89.

10. Gaymard, personal interview.

11. D. Ancona, T. Malone, W. Orlikowski, and P. Senge, "In Praise of the Incomplete Leader," *Harvard Business Review* (February 2007).

12. Personal interview with Philippe Gaud, January 12, 2013.

13. Ibid.

14. J. Godbout and A. Caillé, *L'esprit du don* [The spirit of giving] (Paris: La Découverte and Syros, 2000).

15. D. Ariely, U. Gneezy, G. Loewenstein, and N. Mazar, "Large Stakes and Big Mistakes," *Review of Economic Studies* 76 (2009): 451–469); D. Pink, 2009, *Drive: The Surprising Truth about What Motivates Us* (New York: Riverhead Books, 2009); "Dan Pink: The Puzzle of Motivation," TED Talk, July 2009, http://www.ted.com/talks/dan_pink_on_motivation.html.

16. J. H. Gittell and A. Douglass, "Relational Bureaucracy: Structuring Reciprocal Relationships into Roles," *Academy of Management Review* 37 (October 2012): 709–733.

17. Ibid., 721.

18. Ibid., 715.

19. Personal interview with Apollonia Poilâne, September 12, 2013.

20. Ibid.

21. K. Kamoche and M. Pina e Cunha, "Minimal Structures from Jazz Improvisation to Product Innovation," *Organization Studies* 22, no. 5 (2001): 747.

22. T. Gioia, *The Imperfect Art: Reflections on Jazz and Modern Culture* (New York: Oxford University Press, 1988), 55.

23. K. Weick, "Creativity and the Aesthetics of Imperfection," in *Creative Action in Organizations: Ivory Tower Visions and Real World Voices*, edited by C. M. Ford and D. A. Gioia (Thousand Oaks, CA: Sage, 1995), 187–192. Weick uses the phrase "the aesthetics of imperfection" to discuss the example of jazz, particularly Duke Ellington's leadership in developing his band, and suggests that jazz improvisation builds a different mind-set toward error, transforming it into a continuing struggle for virtue. He presents jazz as a model for organizational theory.

24. F. J. Barrett, "Creativity and Improvisation in Jazz and Organizations: Implications for Organizational Learning," *Organization Science* 9, no. 5 (1998): 606.

25. E. Whelan, S. Parise, J. de Valk, and R. Aalbers, "Creating Employee Networks That Deliver Open Innovation," *MIT Sloan Management Review* 53, no. 1 (Fall 2011): 37–44.

CHAPTER 3

1. Definition of *sense*: "1. a meaning conveyed or intended: IMPORT, SIGNIFI-CATION; *especially*: one of a set of meanings a word or phrase may bear especially as segregated in a dictionary entry. 2a: the faculty of perceiving by means of sense organs. b: a specialized function or mechanism (as sight, hearing, smell, taste, or touch) by which an animal receives and responds to external or internal stimuli. c: the sensory mechanisms constituting a unit distinct from other functions (as movement or thought). 3. Conscious awareness or rationality—usually used in plural <finally came to his *senses*>. 4a: A particular sensation or kind or quality of sensation <a good *sense* of balance>. b: a definite but often vague awareness or impression <felt a *sense* of insecurity> <a *sense* of danger>. c: a motivating aware-ness <a *sense* of shame>. d: a discerning awareness and appreciation <her *sense* of humor>. 5. CONSENSUS <the *sense* of the meeting>. 6a: capacity for effective appli-cation of the powers of the mind as a basis for action or response: INTELLIGENCE. b: sound mental capacity and understanding typically marked by shrewdness and practicality; *also*: agreement with or satisfaction of such power <this decision makes *sense*>. 7. One of two opposite directions especially of motion (as of a point, line, or surface)." *Merriam-Webster's Collegiate Dictionary*, 11th ed., s.v. "sense."

2. K. E. Weick and K. H. Roberts, "Collective Mind in Organizations: Heed-ful Interrelating on Flight Decks," *Administrative Science Quarterly* 38 (1993): 357–381; K. E. Weick, K. M. Sutcliffe, and D. Obstfeld, "Organizing for High Reli-ability: Processes of Collective Mindfulness," *Research in Organizational Behavior* 21 (1999): 81–123; K. E. Weick, K. M. Sutcliffe, and D. Obstfeld, "Organizing and the Process of Sensemaking," *Organization Science* 16, no. 4 (2005): 409–421.

3. J. R. Taylor and E. J. Van Every, *The Emergent Organization: Communi-cation as Its Site and Surface* (Mahwah, NJ: Erlbaum, 2000), 144.

4. R. W. Scott, *Institutions and Organizations* (Thousand Oaks, CA: Sage, 1995).

5. Weick, Sutcliffe, and Obstfeld, "Organizing and the Process of Sensemak-ing," 410.

6. J. H. Gittell and A. Douglass, "Relational Bureaucracy: Structuring Re-ciprocal Relationships into Roles," *Academy of Management Review* 37 (Octo-ber 2012): 708.

7. Weick et al., "Organizing for High Reliability."

8. B. Krause, *The Great Animal Orchestra: Finding the Origins of Music in the World's Wild Places* (New York: Little, Brown, 2012); J. Hoffman, "Q&A: Soundscape Explorer," *Nature* 485 (2012), 308; R. S. Payne and S. McVay, "Songs of Humpback Whales," *Science* 173 (1971): 585–597.

9. C. Hornstrup, J. Loehr-Petersen, J. G. Madsen, T. Johansen, and A. V. Jensen, *Developing Relational Leadership: Resources for Developing Reflexive Organizational Practices* (Chagrin Falls, OH: Taos Institute Publications, 2012).

10. W. Bennis and R. J. Thomas, *Geeks and Geezers: How Era, Values and Defining Moments Shape Leaders* (Boston: Harvard Business School Press, 2002).

11. "Haptonomie," http://www.haptonomie.com/_en/haptonomy/. *Hapto*, from the Greek verb *haptein*, means "I touch, I reunite, I establish a relationship, I attach (myself) to . . ." In the figurative sense it means "I establish (tactilely) a contact so as to make healthy (make whole), to confirm (the other person in his or her existence)."

12. For references on social networks, see B. Wellman and S. D. Berkowitz (eds.), *Social Structures: A Network Approach* (New York: Cambridge University Press, 1988); J. M. Podolny and J. N. Baron, "Resources and Relationships: Social Networks and Mobility in the Workplace," *American Sociological Review* 62, no. 5 (1997): 673–693; A.-L. Barabási, *Linked: How Everything Is Connected to Everything Else and What It Means for Business, Science, and Everyday Life* (New York: Plume, 2003); L. C. Freeman, *The Development of Social Network Analysis: A Study in the Sociology of Science* (Vancouver: Empirical Press, 2004); G. A. Barnett, *Encyclopedia of Social Networks* (Thousand Oaks, CA: Sage, 2011); and C. Kadushin, *Understanding Social Networks: Theories, Concepts, and Findings* (New York: Oxford University Press, 2012).

13. A. Wrzesniewski, C. McCauley, and P. R. Chem, "Odor and Affect: Individual Differences in the Impact of Odor on Liking for Places, Things and People," *Senses* 24, no. 6 (1999): 713–721.

14. P. Senge, *The Fifth Discipline Fieldbook* (New York: Crown, 1994).

15. Karl E. Weick, "The Collapse of Sensemaking in Organizations: The Mann Gulch Disaster," *Administrative Science Quarterly* 38 (1993): 628–652.

CHAPTER 4

1. H. Takeuchi, E. Osono, and N. Shimizu, "The Contradictions That Drive Toyota's Success," *Harvard Business Review* (June 2008), 98.

2. "Alcatel-Lucent Q4 2011 Earnings Call Transcript," February 10, 2012, http://www.morningstar.com/earnings/35224262-alcatellucent-adr-q4-2011.aspx.

3. Ibid.

4. To understand systems thinking and system dynamics, see the following: R. L. Ackoff, *Ackoff's Best: His Classic Writings on Management* (New York: Wiley, 1999); L. Bertalanffy, *General System Theory: Foundations, Development,*

Applications (New York: Braziller, 1969); J. K. Hazy, J. A. Goldstein, and B. B. Lichtenstein, *Complex Systems Leadership Theory: New Perspectives from Complexity Science on Social and Organizational Effectiveness* (Mansfield, MA: ISCE, 2007); D. Meadows, *Thinking in Systems: A Primer* (White River Junction, VT: Chelsea Green, 2008); and P. M. Senge, *The Fifth Discipline: The Art and Practice of the Learning Organization* (New York: Doubleday/Currency, 1990).

5. D. Vera and M. Crossan, "Improvisation and Innovative Performance in Teams," *Organization Science* 16, no. 3 (2005): 203.

6. Ibid.

7. Ibid., 206.

8. R. E. Miles, G. Miles, C. C. Snow, K. Blomqvist, and H. Rocha, "The I-Form Organization," *California Management Review* 51, no. 4 (2009): 61.

9. Ibid., 73. The term *extended enterprise* was introduced by J. Dyer, *Collaborative Advantage: Winning through Extended Enterprise Supplier Networks* (New York: Oxford University Press, 2000).

10. Miles et al., 69.

11. Ibid., 71. See also K. Blomqvist, "Trust in a Dynamic Environment—Fast Trust as a Threshold Condition for Asymmetric Technology Partnership Formation in the ICT Sector," in *Trust under Pressure: Empirical Investigations of Trust and Trust Building in Uncertain Circumstances*, edited by K. Bijlsma and R. K. Woolthuis (Cheltenham, UK: Elgar, 2005), 127–147; and G. von Krogh, "Care in Knowledge Creation," *California Management Review* 40, no. 3 (1998): 133–153.

12. M. De Wit, M. Wade, and E. Schouten, "Hardwiring and Softwiring Corporate Responsibility: A Vital Combination," *Corporate Governance* 6, no. 4 (2006): 491.

13. Ibid., 492.

14. J. Cramer and A. van der Heidjen, A. (2006). "Corporate Social Responsibility as a Tailor-Made Search Process," in *Challenge of Organizing and Implementing Corporate Social Responsibility*, edited by J. Jonker and M. de Witte (New York: Palgrave Macmillan, 2006).

15. De Wit, Wade, and Schouten, "Hardwiring and Softwiring," 495.

16. M. T. Hansen, H. Ibarra, and U. Peyer, "The Best Performing CEOs in the World," *Harvard Business Review* (January–February 2013): 81–95.

CHAPTER 5

1. M. Arndt Kirchhoff, CEO de Kirchhoff Automotive GmbH, private lecture at Veolia seminar, Berlin, June 24, 2012.

2. Ibid.

3. Ibid.

4. R. M. Kanter, "How Great Companies Think Differently," *Harvard Business Review* (November 2011): 66–78.

5. Pernod Ricard's values: entrepreneurship, mutual trust and sense of ethics.

6. Carl Becker, "Mr. Wells and the New History," *American Historical Review* 26, no. 4 (July 1921): 642.

7. J. T. Seaman Jr. and G. D. Smith, "Your Company's History as a Leadership Tool," *Harvard Business Review* (December 2012): 45–52, p. 48.

8. Ibid.

9. Ibid., 51.

10. Christine Lagarde, speech at a conference at HEC Paris, MBA Program, October 19, 2005.

11. T. Zeldin, *Conversation* (London: Harvill, 1998).

12. E. Long Lingo and S. O'Mahony, "Nexus Work: Brokerage on Creative Projects," *Administrative Science Quarterly* 55 (2010): 47–81.

13. Ibid., 74.

14. W. J. Orlikowski, "Knowing in Practice: Enacting a Collective Capability in Distributed Organizing," *Organization Science* 13 (2002): 249.

15. H. Ibarra, M. Kilduff, and W. Tsai, "Zooming In and Out: Connecting Individuals and Collectivities at the Frontiers of Organizational Network Research," *Organization Science* 16 (2005): 367; M. Kilduff and W. Tsai, *Social Networks and Organizations* (London: Sage, 2003).

16. J. M. George, "Creativity in Organizations," *Academy of Management Annals* 1 (2008): 467.

17. Long Lingo and Mahony, "Nexus Work," 52.

18. Ibid.

19. Ibid., Table 2, p. 59.

20. J. H. Gittell and A. Douglass, "Relational Bureaucracy: Structuring Reciprocal Relationships into Roles," *Academy of Management Review* 37 (October 2012): 716.

21. Personal interview with Apollonia Poilâne, September 12, 2013.

CHAPTER 6

1. The protocol has been tested in both corporate settings (leadership development programs) and educational settings (master's, MBA, and EMBA programs) with more than seven hundred individuals. Feedback from these early experiments

(2009–2013) shows that perception, reliance, resilience, and responsibility are the keys to increase confidence, collaboration, and trust to foster innovation and generate business that builds sense for the organization and its employees. Sense relationality unfolds a new paradigm that combines relational leadership with sense building. Introspection, conversation, resilience, and responsible leadership action plans are the four pillars of the savoir-relier protocol.

On the subject of perception, 92 percent of participants responded positively on the distinctive value of seeing and observing versus thinking/interpreting and imagining/feeling; 85 percent found listening, discerning sounds, voices, and words for what they were versus what they wanted to hear, a useful exercise.

On the subject of self-confidence, 92 percent of participants found the savoir-relier introspective work a powerful tool to grow their self-awareness and confidence, with some declaring they had started applying the self-portrait with their spouse or partner to transfer their self-understanding to their personal sphere.

On the subject of interpersonal relationships or reliance, 95 percent of participants found a positive impact of conversation on their ability to interact with others, including subordinates and bosses, talking about "improving the quality of their understanding of the other and of themselves."

On the subject of resilience, 75 percent found the exercise useful to grow their capacity to face difficult and complex issues, and 46 percent said they needed more time to practice story searching.

2. Merriam-Webster's Collegiate Dictionary, 11th ed., s.v. "courage."

3. T. Zeldin, An Intimate History of Humanity (New York: Random House, 1994).

CHAPTER 7

1. M. Uhl-Bien and R. Marion, *Complexity Leadership* (Charlotte, NC: Information Age, 2007); M. Uhl-Bien and S. M. Ospina, *Advancing Relational Leadership Research: A Dialogue among Perspectives* (Charlotte, NC: Information Age, 2012). Using a complexity frame, relational leadership scholars offer a move from an individual, top-down, heroic leadership approach to a collective, distributed, or emergent leadership model; they look into networks that are heterogeneous and present new methods that capture the intricacies of complex leadership dynamics.

2. Figures of speech in poetry involve many different devices that enrich language by building associations between words. *Metonymy* is an association of words in which reference to something or someone is made by naming one of its attributes (contiguity). A *metaphor* is a term or phrase that is applied to something to which it is not literally applicable in order to suggest a resemblance (similarity).

3. E. Catmull, "How Pixar Fosters Creativity," *Harvard Business Review* (September 2008): 66.

4. Aristotle, "On the Art of Poetry," in *The Poetic*, trans. I. Bywater, with a preface by G. Murray (n.p., 1905).

5. E. Morin, "Beyond Determinism: The Dialogue of Order and Disorder," *SubStance* 40 (1983): 22–35; E. Morin, *La complexité humaine* [Human complexity] (Paris: Flammarion, 1994), 3–15; E. Morin, *On Complexity* (Cresskill, NJ: Hampton Press, 2008).

6. L. Heracleous, "A Comment on the Role of Metaphor in Knowledge Generation," *Academy of Management Review* 28, no. 2 (2003): 190.

7. G. Lakoff, "A Contemporary Theory of Metaphor," in *Metaphor and Thought*, 2nd ed., edited by A. Ortony (New York: Cambridge University Press, 1993), 203–251.

8. L. D. Griffin, "Walt Whitman's Voice," *Walt Whitman Quarterly Review* 9, no. 3 (Winter 1992): 125–133.

9. V. Gauthier, "Theoretical and Practical Approach to Poetic Translation," PhD dissertation, Sorbonne University, Paris, 1994.

10. P. Eluard, *Donner à voir* [Giving to see] (Paris: Gallimard, 1939), 131–132 (my translation).

11. Y. Bonnefoy, "On the Translation of Form in Poetry," in *World Literature Today* 53, no. 3 (1979) (quoting J. Brodsky), 146.

12. G. Wagner, *Selected Poems of Charles Baudelaire* (New York: Grove Press, 1974).

13. R. Jakobson, *Closing Statements: Linguisitics and Poetics in Style in Language*, edited by T. Sebeok (Cambridge, MA: MIT Press, 1960).

14. U. Eco, *Dire presque la même chose: Expériences de traduction* [Saying almost the same thing: experiences in translation], trans. M. Bouzaher (Paris: Grasset, 2001).

15. V. Gauthier, *Poetic Translation of* New Fires, *Neo-epic Poem, by L. D. Griffin*, master's thesis, University of Paris III, Sorbonne, 1986.

16. Gauthier, "Theoretical and Practical Approach to Poetic Translation," 258.

17. J. H. Gittell and A. Douglass, "Relational Bureaucracy: Structuring Reciprocal Relationships into Roles," *Academy of Management Review* 37 (October 2012): 709–733.

18. Ibid., 722.

19. Ibid., 724.

20. Gauthier, "Theoretical and Practical Approach to Poetic Translation," 258. The word is borrowed from the terminology of Henri Meschonnic in *Pour*

la poétique, Tome I [For poetics] (Paris: Gallimard, Le chemin, 1970). He argues that poetic translation is founded on the interaction between theory and practice and poses the homogeneity of translating and writing or "reading-writing." Poetic translation produces a text with its ambivalence and its conflicts and establishes a relationship between the source text and the intertextuality of the translator that he calls "the writing of a reading-writing" which recreates a *"forme-sens"* (meaning-form).

Italic page numbers indicate material in figures and tables.